Radical Desire

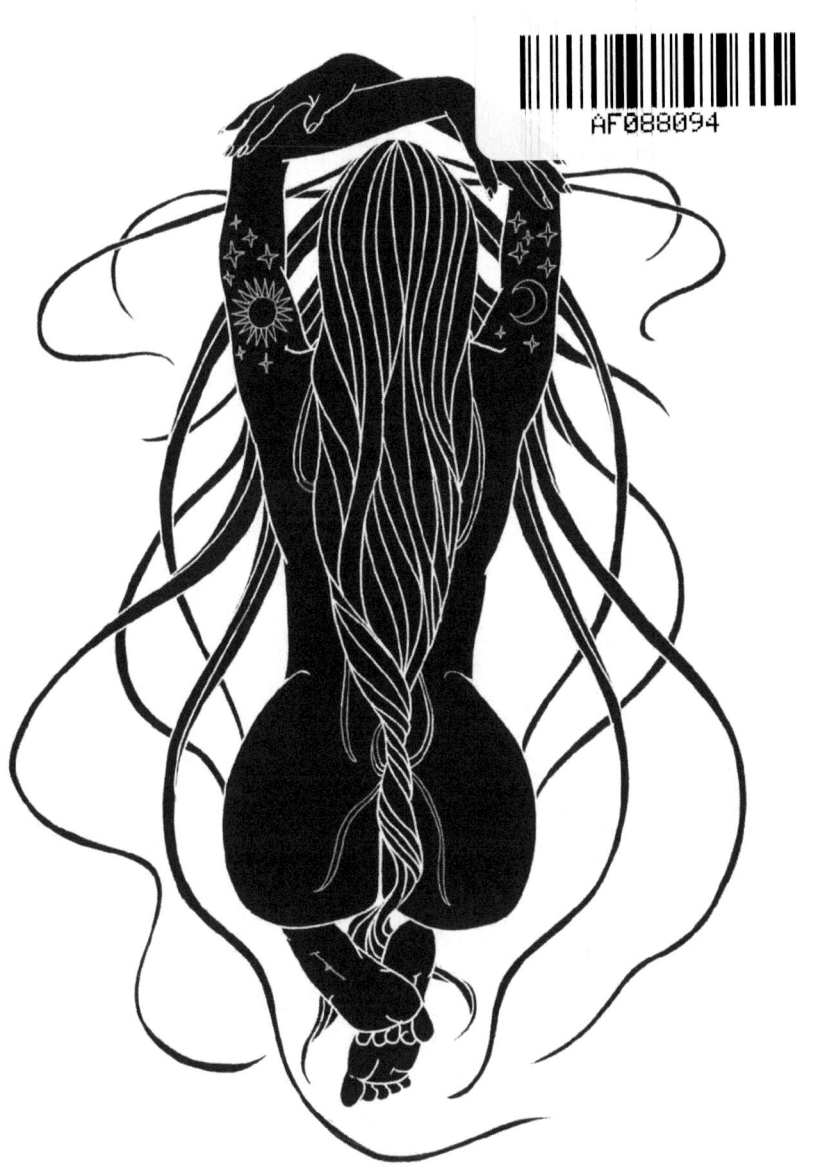

Radical Desire

Kink & Magickal Sex

by
Mark Ramsden
& Ruth Ramsden

Mandrake

Copyright © Mark Ramsden, Ruth Ramden 2012
2nd considerably expanded edition

All rights reserved. No part of this work may be reproduced or utilized in any form by any means electronic or mechanical, including *xerography, photocopying, microfilm,* and *recording,* or by any information storage system without permission in writing from the author.

Published by
Mandrake of Oxford
PO Box 250
OXFORD
OX1 1AP (UK)
ISBN 978-1-906958-19-0

Contents

Introduction 9
The Way In 11
The Death of Sado-Masochism. If Only… 12
Safe Words 18
Adult Babies 19
An Evening At The Torture Garden 20
Piercing 27
Corsets 39
Rubber 44
Sex Accessories 46
Bisexuality 49
Footnote 52
Switching 53
Shakespeare And Radical Desire 57
The Dark Side Of Tantric Sex 61
Fetish Sex Work 69
Radical Desire And Media Disinformation 75
Scarification 82
The Law Of Diminishing Returns 84
What Trina Said 84
My Lord Lucifer 88
To The Devil A Daughter 90

FallenAngelBrewery.com 91

Sex Toys 93

Lovehoney.co.uk 94

Reggie Kray And Little Freddie 95

Vampire Eroticism:
Rapidly Gaining Ascendency On The Scene 97

For Your Arse Only:
Ian Fleming and Kink 98

Gordon Brown -
A case for non-erotic asphyxiation 100

The Abba Test 104

The Rimming Machine 106

Short Stories
Nick/'Nicola' 108

Mr Strict - The Diary of a Corrective Therapist 121

Madam Petra 128

21st Century Eddie Drood
– Charles Dickens Remixed 135

The Meaning Of Life 137

Some of the activities discussed in this book are potentially dangerous. It is essential to be certain of any partner's mental and physical health before surrendering control to them.

Introduction

Radical Desire blends sex, religion, violence, taboo-busting, risk and ritual. It's hardly surprising that more and more people are joining the throng. This adrenalin-kick activity is not only about hedonism, (although it is if you're doing it right...) there is often much anguish along the way - partly because of the constraints imposed by the Christian religion and partly because of the myths propagated by the therapy industry. Sex play with multiple partners is 'wrong' apparently. Odd, that, as it's been going on since the dawn of time. And monogamous romance tends to fail eventually however much one tries, often desperately hard, in the case of shared children, or more cynically for the mortgage or just to appear respectable. Exploring Kink is not an easy path to tread. You're just as likely to uncover severe psychic wounds, as experience ecstasy but it's all part of the long road to the palace of wisdom. Sexual healing easily beats paying some idiot shrink for half-remembered Freud, where, in the immortal words of Frasier's Daphne Moon, it doesn't matter whether you get better or not. It's certainly more fun than attempting to suppress your urges with the chemical cosh of legal tranquillisers, anti depressants, or whatever they're pushing currently, generally bribed by Big Pharma.

Despite the recent media avalanche of sexual explicitness, the battle for sexual freedom is far from won. Many otherwise liberal people still confuse S/M play/kinky sex/radical desire with abuse. It is actually a reaction to abuse, an attempt to heal a deep wound. The powers that be are still attempting to promote the idea that heterosexual sex within marriage is superior to the many other forms of sexual pleasure, even at a time when fewer people manage to live up to this often unattainable ideal.

The Way In

If you're still wondering whether to join in and don't fancy night clubs, online cruising or contact mags then a 'Munch' or a Fetish Fair is often the best way to meet potential local partners. You see clearly what you might be getting rather than trusting to luck. And you will be able to hear an indecent proposal in a pub or restaurant rather than the great sound of Hard House, banging away from decade to decade. Well, I quite liked that, being an incorrigible E head, and we may as well mention drugs here as many scene players find it easier to bond on MDMA which gets you 'loved up' with people far easier than chat up lines or awkward silences.

To those who find the tone of parts of this books flippant, I would answer that scene players are usually light-hearted individuals. They are generally more concerned with enjoyment than dry theorising. Writing about Radical Desire, *especially* when called BDSM, is often dark and doomy but it would be a shame to ignore the humorous aspects of adult sexual play. It would also be inaccurate and misleading. Some of the games adults play may end in tears but most participants in these activities are familiar with the sound of laughter. We offer this book in the hope that those with the courage to defy convention also find ecstasy and enlightenment at the end of their journey.

NB It's probably best to dip in and out of this book although masochists and pain sluts may wish to endure the entire text in one go.

The Death of Sado-Masochism. If Only…

Leaving aside the glamour of the forbidden, there is no doubt that the term Sado-Masochism has a pejorative ring to it. This may be because it was formulated by Krafft-Ebing, writing at the end of the nineteenth century when repressive Christian morality was even more prevalent than it is today. 'Psychopathia Sexualis', his account of a number of sexual paraphilias, is littered with words like 'loathsome' and 'disgusting', hardly appropriate adjectives for a supposedly dispassionate observer. In addition, most of his theories have not stood the test of time. His cures, including electric shock treatment, are often misguided. He was, however, the first to use the term sado-masochism, in itself a mixed blessing.

There was no particularly logical reason to yoke together two writers who may have achieved immortality but are not necessarily representative of their eponymous conditions. The Marquis de Sade was driven by fantasies of coercing unwilling victims and inflicting extremes of pain upon them, whereas Sacher-Masoch was obsessed by the need for a code of conduct for dominant/submissive behaviour. Fortunately, it is this latter view that has prevailed, at least in fetish clubs and in most currently available commercial erotica. Whatever activities scene players may indulge in, most follow this rule: 'The only perversion is coercion'.

In any case, few would now describe themselves as being either a sadist or a masochist. Currently terminology would usually be dominant or submissive or, in American usage, top and bottom – although this ignores the many who like to explore both roles. Just as describing someone as homosexual, bisexual or heterosexual is to ignore the shifting

sands of sexuality, it is inaccurate and misleading to think of oneself as either dominant or submissive. Even those who are happy to be described at one end of the spectrum often find themselves hankering to see how the other side lives as the years go by. If I had a pound for every implacable Mistress who is secretly a switch I'd have...twenty to thirty quid, enough for a new pair of rubber knickers perhaps. Unfortunately the granite-faced tedium of thermonuclear Fem Dom has the most market share currently, egged on by the sad sub worm-men who need more and more degradation each time.

The Marquis de Sade may possess a certain dark glamour but his coercive ideas taint all forms of radical desire, at least for the general public. He was nurtured by a libertine priest and some of his former mistresses; his mother decamped to a convent where she was to spend the rest of her days. His Dad's hobby was shooting at random passers by. We can say, without fear of contradiction, that he was badly parented. Once incarcerated in the Bastille by a vengeful mother in law, de Sade wrote frantically while under sentence of death. It's hardly surprising that much of his writing is truly transgressive – he had little to lose.

Although his writing is intentionally revolting, it should be pointed out that he did not use the death penalty when appointed a judge and never killed or tortured anyone even though his aristocratic status gave him freedom from prosecution. At a time when the streets were literally running with blood this is surely proof that the Marquis used writing to exorcise the demons inside him, in preference to acting out the horrific events he imagined.

Although Sacher-Masoch is more acceptable to contemporary readers, due to his emphasis on consensual activity, his work lacks the power of de Sade's writing. Perhaps because Sacher-Masoch was able to live out his fantasies he was not driven to invent manic extremes of cruelty.

De Sade's writing is often merely a list of the worst atrocities he could imagine. Although academic theorists remain fond of using his work as a springboard for their own concerns it is probably fair to say that de Sade's books are likely to be bought because of his notoriety rather than the pleasure anyone gets from actually reading these turgid and repetitive texts.

In contrast, Sacher-Masoch's desire for female domination is now almost respectable (although his fur fetish is currently beyond the pale). His writing also resounds with occult references which may have helped bring to a wider audience the correlation between Goddess worship and female domination, no longer a secret known only to those concerning themselves with what was once called black magic.

It may be unrealistic to try to discourage the use of the term 'sadomasochism' but, as it carries so much negative baggage, it would indeed be better to find some other language to describe these activities.

An accurate term free of negativity is 'power exchange sex', which has achieved some acceptance in America. 'Kinky' or just 'Kink" is a naughty but nice word without all the dread overtones of 'fetishistic', which at the time of writing has been misused so often that it now conjures up either models in shiny rubber or criminal activity up to and including serial killing.

Fakir Musafar has coined 'body play' (also the influential concept of 'modern primitives'), which seems to encapsulate most of the areas already discussed, as does 'fetishism' itself – although is already be irreversibly tainted by its pathological connotations. Incidentally I was pierced by Fakir Musafa, who was hoping to open my Mulhadra Chakra, (with a perineum ring). There's times when I'm mystical and times when

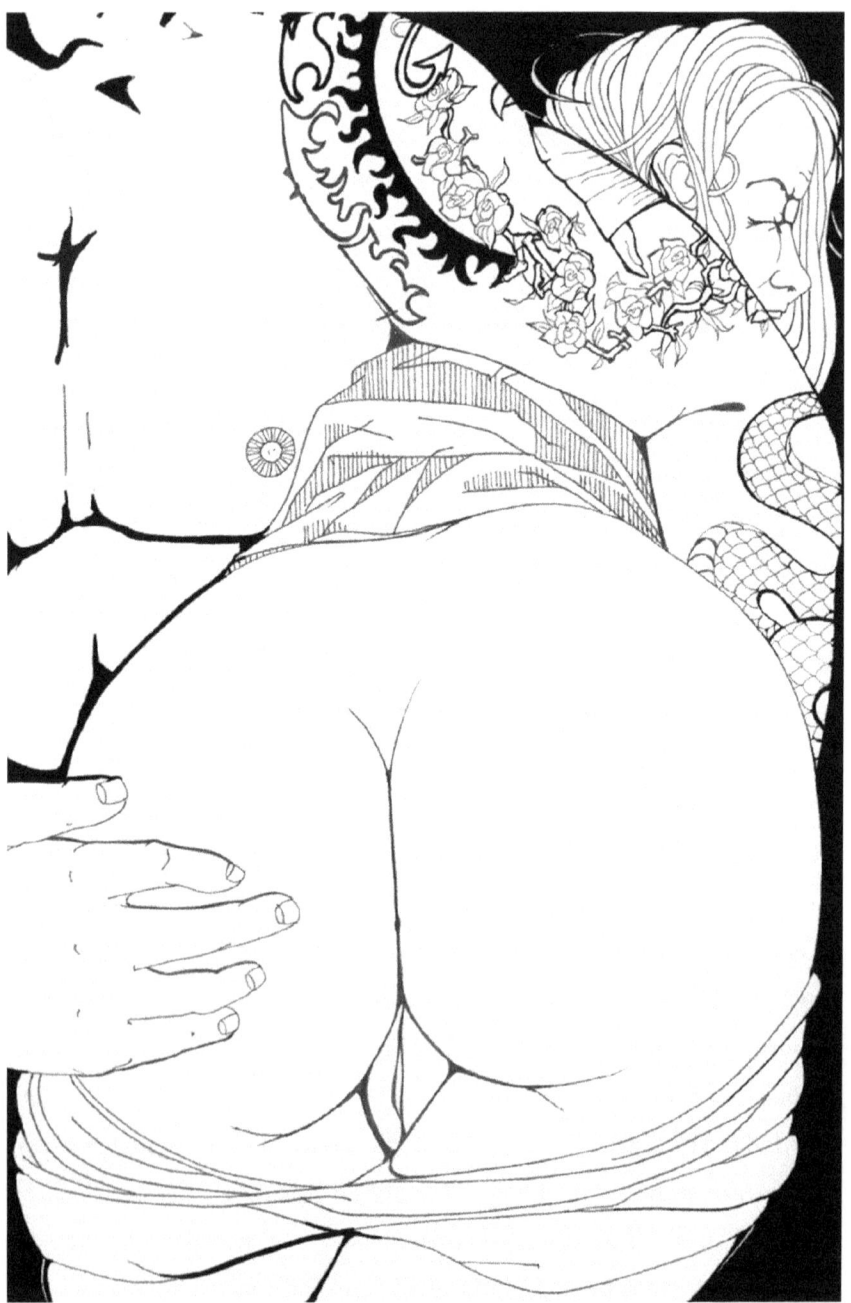

I'm not. For whatever reason, perhaps because I'd already been pierced there not to mention fucked by some men and many women with a strap-on, maybe this procedure wasn't necessary, whatever, the earth didn't move. However he remains one of the Body Art movement's greatest Shamans. I was amused when the great man, (in truth a great pioneer whose work must be seen to be believed) asked the time, one of his minions gave it and he said, "We're an hour late. That's just about right." Silly Fakir. (Before you start, I greatly admire his extreme body modification rituals which this innovative artist invented some time in the fifties.)

Radical Desire, for the purposes of this book, means magickal sexual behaviour that seeks to transform. The dictionary definition of radical offers a number of choices, two of which are highly apposite. Fundamental – in the sense that the desire to seek out new avenues of sexual ecstasy is deeply embedded in every human being. This includes the need to confront both the divine and the dark side of ourselves. Intrinsic – these desires are embedded deep within us all.

These are not new ideas but the Christian derived hatred of the body and the darker aspects of our spirituality has resulted in repression of our most natural instincts. The first step towards gaining wider acceptance for this sexuality would be to refrain from using the language of psychiatrists and criminologists for adult consensual behaviour. In this context, terms such as 'deviance' or 'perversion' should be consigned to the dustbin of history. (Although some scene players delight in calling themselves 'perves', in a similar manner to the way 'queer' has been reclaimed by gay activists.) At the very least the word enthusiast could be substituted for fetishist. As most people wish to repeat pleasurable experiences, and sometimes keep mementoes of these events, we could all be described as fetishists. The millions of men who gawp at breasts in tabloid newspapers are not described as breast fetishists; the term is used to demonise.

Restricting the use of terms such as sado-masochism and fetishism may seem as doomed as lexicographer Eric Partridge's attempt to have the Marquis de Sade known as Comte de Sade, but the use of inaccurate and derogatory language derived from obsolete academic studies prevents more people from experiencing the positive and transformative aspects of Kink. There may be people who can only experience sexual ecstasy with an aubergine but many scene people and private individuals also experience state-sanctioned forms of sex alongside our more radical enthusiasms. We experience love, sexual intercourse, raise children. Why should we be stigmatised by the label fetishist?

Why cling on to the language of nineteenth century psychopathology? It is time to bury the negative legacy of Krafft-Ebing and the Marquis de Sade.

Safe Words

Apologists for sado-masochism usually make much of the safeword convention. This is a word which will stop whatever is going on immediately. Until a safeword is spoken a submissive partner has the choice of pleading or begging for release without the dominant having to take any notice. Partners sensitive to each other's limits shouldn't really need safewords but to say such a thing usually attracts angry letters and telephone calls. The point is they don't always work anyway. Even experienced players still manage to injure themselves occasionally if an endorphin rush makes them insensitive to the damage being inflicted by a whip or a cane. As corporal punishment enthusiasts are keen on pushing pain barriers such injuries are hardly unknown. As in most sports, accidents can happen. (Corporal punishment scenarios are best enjoyed after warming the skin up gradually. This reduces marking of the flesh and greatly increases the pleasure for both parties.)

A young woman recently miscalculated the damage to her bottom during a caning and had to visit Casualty when she started losing significant amounts of blood and lymph fluid. After a surprising number of hospital staff had made an excuse to come and see the damage, she was x-rayed and bandaged up, using the newer type moist dressing which heals much quicker. "Why didn't you stop?" she was asked, over and over again – a reasonable question. "Endorphins," she replied.

As safe words will not protect anyone who is in an ecstatic trance, it really should be up to the dominant partner to be careful at these moments of bliss and transcendence. To quote Celia Tan's brilliant title for one of her SF/SM books, (Circlet Press), 'Telepaths Don't Need Safewords'. We can't all be telepathic but we can be watching carefully to make sure that skin is not scarred for life and that submissive partners are as safe as they can be.

Adult Babies

Adult babies usually inspire ridicule, naturally enough as the disparity between what these (almost invariably) men experience and what they look like to outsiders is often striking. Many have lost their hair and they have usually acquired enough fat to resemble an overgrown baby.

Despite first impressions adult babies are far from passive, they are usually in control of whoever is playing the part of their mothers. This is topping from the bottom, supposedly a heinous sin, if you're a vengeful Domme who always has to be on top, but why shouldn't submissives be in charge if they prefer this mode?

Whatever the pecking order, and Mother often does know best, these role-players have decided to re-visit their original trauma – with the difference that this time they are in charge.

An Evening At The Torture Garden

The Torture Garden is the best known Fetish Club in London, arguably the best known and indeed the best in the world, having built up an enviable reputation as a club which combines radical sex, fashion, dance music and performance art. Although patrons expect to be shocked occasionally, some of the club's loyal followers felt that the requiem for Anton La Vey, the founder of the church of Satan, was perhaps a little too cutting edge for comfort. Some not particularly prudish or conservative clubbers were wary of any demonic energies that might be unleashed by a certain self proclaimed sorcerer who hosted the evening. This was some time lost in my twenty years intense clubbing, probably mid 90s. This man was not one of those who would wish to make s/m respectable by hymning the praises of consensual adult activity and stressing the need for previously agreed safewords to protect the submissive partner. So it was with some trepidation that I swallowed a small amount of psycho-active mushrooms and made my way to the Torture Garden where the guests were greeted with a sprinkling of water from a number of hooded acolytes. I can't say my aura was significantly cleansed by this and, as I was soon being quizzed by a cheap and cheerful camera crew from a late night programme designed specifically for drunken men gathered around takeaway cartons, the ritual banishment was obviously missing a crucial incantation or two.

 I soon gravitated to the dungeon area where many of the assembled congregation were coating their skin with propane then setting it briefly alight, an eye opener at the time although, like many other once extreme activities, now just another transitory thrill.

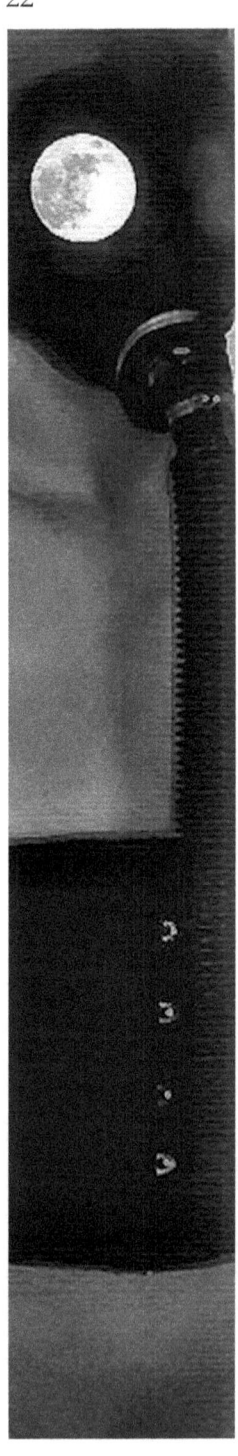

Nearby were priestesses administering to the needs of their flock. If the various whippings, canings and sound thrashings on offer palled you could also watch charming Oriental bondage displays, visit the fetish market and watch Kenneth Anger's 'Lucifer Rising' in an appropriately demonic atmosphere. Hocus-pocus films don't really bother me under normal circumstances but, with the handful of magic mushrooms beginning to make themselves felt, and a particularly savage joyless whipping being dealt out by an unpleasant man right next to the screen, I was starting to feel uncomfortable. One of the stars of Lucifer Rising was Donald Cammell, one of the creators of psychedelic-noir classic Performance, who eventually killed himself – yet another whose dark dabblings seem to have done more harm than good. The fate of some of those who were involved with La Vey (Jayne Mansfield and Susan Anson, one of the Manson murderers) would also seem to prove that 'superstition can sometimes bring bad luck' - used by Umberto Ecco to introduce Foucault's Pendulum. (And borrowed by myself in a much less erudite but considerably more amusing murder mystery trilogy set in the fetish scene.)

By now, progress through the club was occasionally hazardous due to the many women who wore horns and spiked neck collars. Although

I hesitate to invoke Frank Spencer in this company, they could easily have had someone's eye out.

Our host for the satanic invocation finally appeared on stage at one a.m., looking elegantly cadaverous in a Harlequin costume based on the Chaos Magic eight-arrow sigil. A nude woman was tethered to an alter as we waited for the appearance of the cloven-footed one. It was here that the attention started to wander as various demons were summoned and dispatched. For much of this time I had the choice of looking at the barely fleshed skull of our host or at a nearby woman whose outfit consisted entirely of fishnet stockings. I must confess that there were times when those on stage lost out, especially as the long, incomprehensible invocation meandered on interminably. The problem with Satanic invocations is that they tend to involve the Enochian keys or some sort of gibberish that the merely human can't understand. I was soon wishing that I was doing something other than watching the lanky skeletal figure bellowing something or other into a microphone when I could have been home with a nice cup of organic green tea. I once visited this man to obtain some alternative herbal remedies, when he lived on a grim estate in a hovel patrolled by a Rottweiler. Lovely. I was then editing Fetish Times and was eager to learn from scene veterans. He answered a query about uniforms by appearing in a teachers gown and mortar board, waving a plastic cane and asking if I wanted to be tethered to his Black and Decker Workmate. "Come on! You know you want it!" he bellowed, a most erroneous assumption. In short, watch your step, whatever the scene says about boundaries and safe play there's plenty of sadistic users who will always believe their own bullshit.

Back at the Satanic Mass the accompanying music sounded genuinely diabolical; tortuous electric violin playing and the occasional pummelling of a large gong although at one point there was the welcome

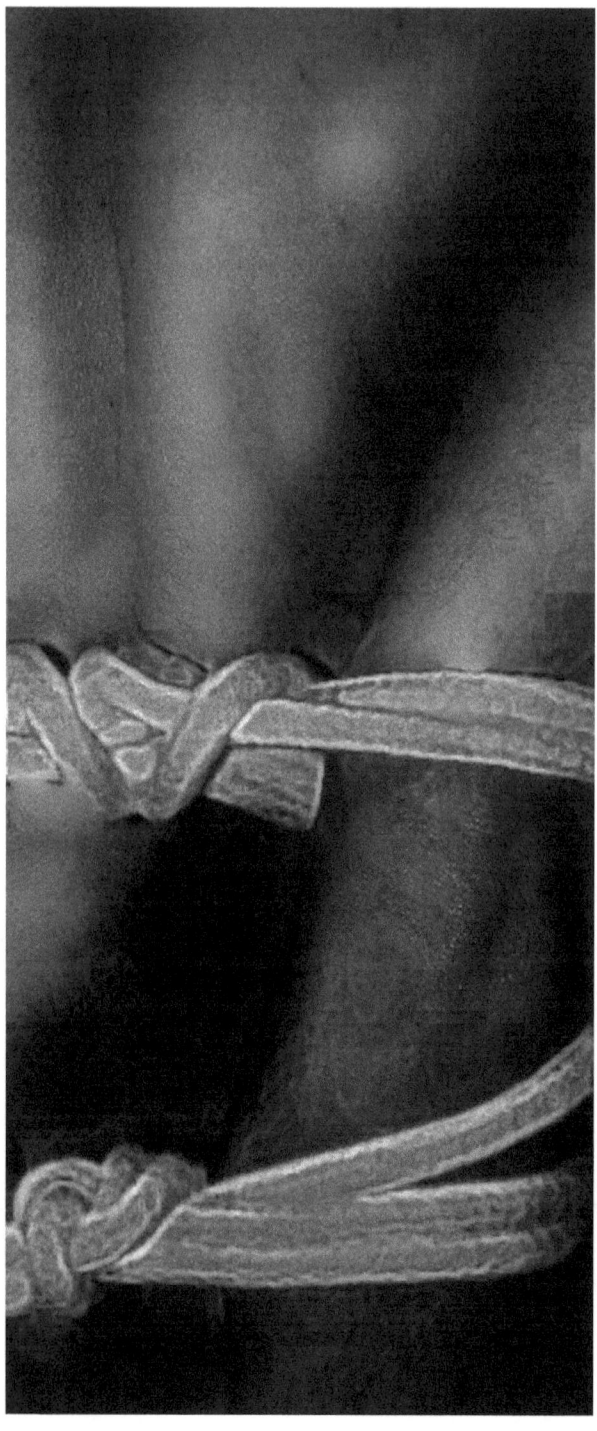

appearance of the renowned glove puppet Sooty. Ho fucking Ho. This 'Chaos Clown' jest added a little light relief but very soon we were back to nothing very much occurring, at least not down here, as opposed to on the astral plane. But that's invocations for you – a long wait and sometimes no-one shows up. In this case the final appearance of Lucifer proved to be worth waiting for. The Prince of Darkness was heralded by a shadow on the backcloth before manifesting triumphantly and having his way with the woman tethered to the altar. It may just have been a man in a realistic rubber Devil suit, as some sceptics claimed, but the fiendish rogering brought proceedings to an end on an appropriately climactic note.

The Torture Garden is justly famous for its mix of dancers, artists, craftspersons, fashion obsessives, sex maniacs and voyeurs. It must be experienced, preferably more than once but eventually the law of diminishing returns applies. Perhaps this applies to the club scene as a whole. Maybe five or six years is enough. Although it took me twenty to pack it in and, if I had enough money I'd probably still be at it, but I'd rather behave badly at private parties or at home. You can always simulate the clubbing experience by making yourself queue for everything putting HARD HOUSE ANTHEMS VOL 99 on at 130 decibels and overcharging yourself for drinks.

You may find sex, fun, excitement, transgression, thrills and spills but: "You are unlikely to find love", in the view of one scene veteran, although some couples do find each other and retire to nest. I did. But my first marriage imploded under the strain of sex and drug addiction, the days you need to recover from lack of sleep and MDMA, ketamine, acid, hash etc and the almost inevitable adultery once the marital handbrake is taken off. The pain resulting from these separations is infinitely more than the pleasure clubbing affords but then...maybe it would have happened anyway? Whatever, once children arrive it no longer looks so sensible to stay up all night and the use of even soft drugs becomes harder to justify. I was stupid enough to ignore this and paid the price, and am still paying it.

Here the gay man or woman without children has considerable advantage and can continue the clubbing lifestyle for much longer. But even for them there eventually comes a time when elitism, noise, cliquishness and high prices become wearisome. And in any case, human beings tire of even the most exquisite pleasures and sensations. ('It's not as good as it used to be', is a familiar mantra on the mainstream club scene.)

Having said that, those who wish to play rather than preen may be better advised to seek out private parties designed with the express purpose of sexual interaction. It's also a good tip for those wishing to preserve their hearing. They will still be able to hear an offering of a whipping years after hardcore clubbers will be bellowing into each others' ear trumpets.

Piercing

Despite the recent fashion for piercing the majority of people are still not particularly keen on the idea of having cold steel threaded through their genitals. This would be understandable except that it is often the same people who think nothing of injuring themselves on the sports field or of consuming enormous amounts of alcohol on a nightly basis. And although I might be heavily pierced I wouldn't dream of undergoing the sort of body modification achieved by the average D.I.Y. enthusiast armed with an electric drill.

Piercing originated in so-called primitive cultures to adorn the body, to enhance sexual pleasure and to mark rites of passage. There are references in the Hindu sacred text, the Kama Sutra, to primitive techniques of piercing the genitals to enhance sensitivity but it is only recently that the practice has become more established in developed societies. While there has never been a better time than the present to experience the many benefits of these adornments caution is still advised. Even a Local Authority certificate that the premises have been inspected is no guarantee that a piercer is competent and individual reactions to piercing are varied. Some people have been known to faint, especially in the Summer months, but most people experience heightened energy and awareness for at least the rest of the day and the pleasure one takes in the expansion of one's body capacity for sensual enjoyment will stay for the rest of one's life. Should anyone be unhappy with a piercing for whatever reason, the flesh will heal quickly once the stud or ring is removed - although my perineum is still minutely ridged due to two horrible piercings that didn't take, maybe because I'm not a tribal type wearing a sarong and giving it plenty of fresh air, this is hardly a tragedy.

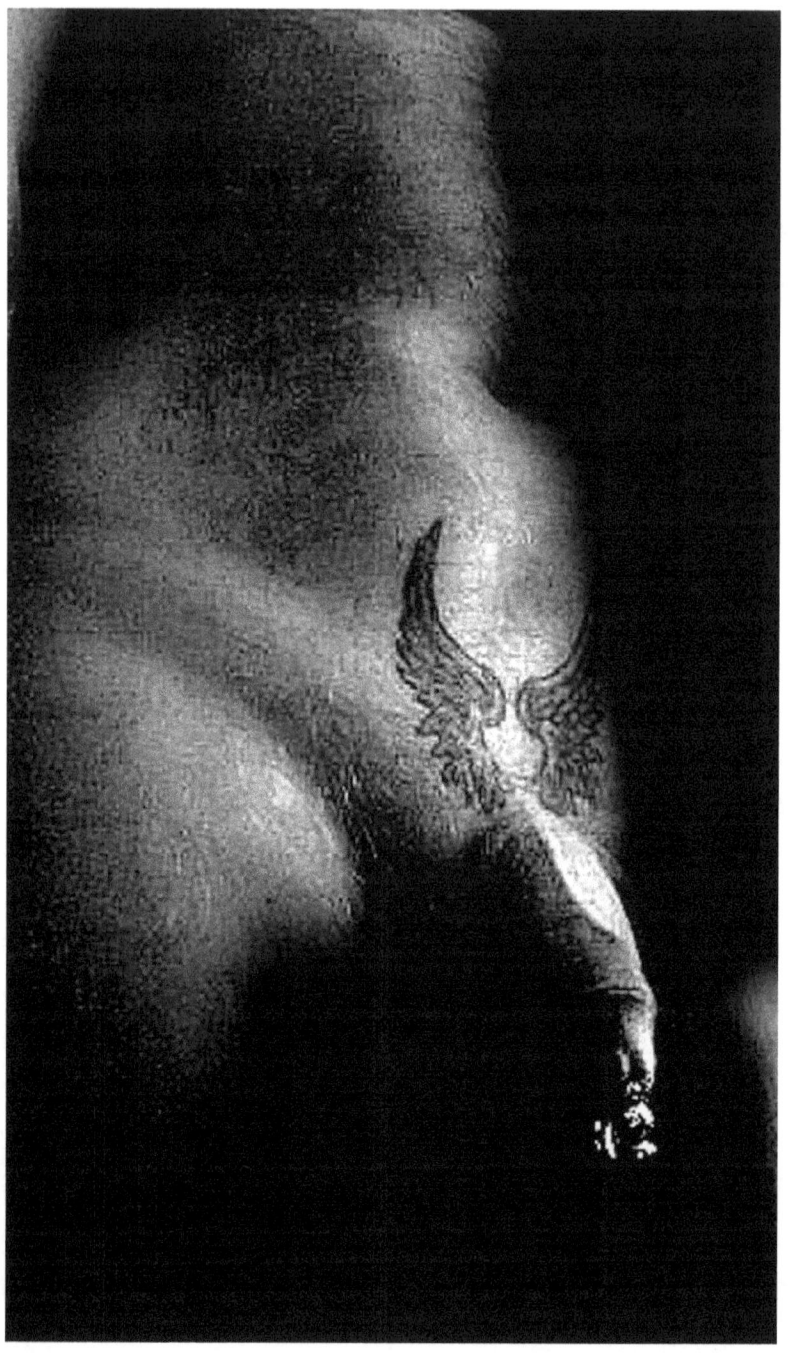

The author making a dick of himself with his eighth Prince Albert upgrade

If it works you can pull the ring to enhance sex play but...the Goddess just didn't want this one to happen.

Those who have piercings are very familiar with a particular question from those who remain unpierced: "Does it hurt?" In general, the initial pain of piercing is quickly over and one can learn to appreciate the rush of energy that results once the body's natural defences against pain start to kick in. Some piercings, even genital ones, are so quick that the job is done before the pain has registered. Stomach and nipple piercings can be much more painful and may also require a long healing time. Regardless of whether it has this effect or not, individuals reaction to pain differs and the skill of the piercer plays a part, making it hard to generalise.

Although there are anaesthetics available for the squeamish many purists prefer using the body's natural resources. Besides, the freeze of the spray on anaesthetic is often uncomfortable, it really is better just to breathe deeply, stay calm and ride the pain out.

The most commonly sought male piercing is the Prince Albert, which is through the eye of the penis and out through the underside of the glans. Men with a foreskin are pierced slightly to one side of the frenum, the loose fold of flesh that connect the foreskin to the penis, whereas a circumcised man can be perforated directly below the glans. A stainless steel ring is then threaded through the opening. Some say the Prince Albert was invented by Beau Brummel to keep the penis flat against the leg in the era of tight trousers when this was known as a dressing ring. It is also claimed that Queen Victoria's consort wore one but the Prince Albert in question is more likely to have been Prince Albert Victor, Duke of Clarence, who was known for a keen interest in all manner of debauchery. According to American piercing expert Doug

Malloy, 'The procedure is quick; the pain, minimal; the healing, rapid; and the pleasure, lifelong.'

It will still take weeks before intercourse is possible but sex play is possible during this time and careful masturbation is possible from day one. It might indeed be difficult to refrain from checking out the new possibilities afforded by genital adornment. Men who play with their genitals before they were pierced will find the process much more pleasurable afterwards.

Although nipple and stomach piercings can be a little troublesome, the Prince Albert is surprisingly painless and the antiseptic action of urine will keep it clean for you. Mr Sebastian, a pioneer piercer who has passed on, recommended quite a long healing time before sexual use but I feel this errs on the side of caution. I know of several reprobates who played with their brand new Prince Alberts the day they were put in, such as myself, but it is recommended that you wait two weeks before erection and another two weeks before orgasm. If you must play with your new piercing wash your hands first, or even better, use a condom. Don't clean it too often or use scented soaps, a saline solution is best, and it is wise to refrain from swimming for the first month or so. Zinc and Vitamin C may speed up the healing process; both supplements are worth taking in any case, as is a regular course of ginseng. Refraining from drink and drugs will strengthen the immune system and bolster the body's natural capacity for healing itself. If you feel the need for an antiseptic, some people use tea tree oil and almond oil in equal parts.

My nipple piercings fell out and eventually I stopped replacing them because men's nipples are a bit boring really, and it gives cretinous tops yet another reason to assume you're a sub but I've still got my eighth upgrade Prince Albert. It took seventeen years from my initiation to journey through thicker and thicker rings till I reached the heaviest I can bear. This one is large enough to have to be welded shut. It can't fall out, an occasional problem with smaller screwed in rings. Loss of a piercing necessitates a quick as possible dash to the nearest body art specialist. You certainly don't want the flesh to heal up having gone to all that effort. I was dumb enough, a bell end you might say, to do the last two stages of my Prince Albert process in one go, having thought that I was used to this sort of thing. What could go wrong? In no time my life partner Ruth Ramsden, who has illustrated this book, and is also an author, and infinitely patient with buffoons, was getting increasingly drunken phone calls consisting almost entirely of "My knob HURTS!" I'd fallen off the wagon to numb the pain, an especially dumb thing for a chronic alcoholic to do. But that's the deep end, the first Prince Albert really doesn't hurt, heals quickly and you'll be as happy as a dog with two dicks, or indeed a man with a penis upgrade.

For some unknown reason I had imagined that it would be easier to have my nipples pierced and had these done first, thinking that if I could cope with this, I would then progress to a Prince Albert (P.A). In actual fact the pain involved in acquiring a P.A is absolutely minimal and the procedure is very quick, whereas the area of flesh to be pierced is much greater in the case of a nipple and the discomfort is correspondingly greater. Having said that, it is still quick and as nothing compared to a lengthy session at the dentist. Perhaps the hardest part of the preparation process for a genital piercing is struggling against cultural conditioning which decrees that we shall not adorn our bodies and that sexual enjoyment for its own sake is in some way wrong.

The ampallang piercing, as recommended in the Kama Sutra and highly prevalent in the areas around the Indian Ocean, is gaining popularity in the West as it give sexual pleasure to both partners. The piercing is right through the head of the penis and feels like a heavy bruising sensation. There may be some discomfort as this settles down. Healing times vary considerably and as some piercers recommend waiting six months before sexual intercourse not many people persevere with this piercing. Few piercers are qualified to perform this operation and, as it is potentially lethal, extreme caution is recommended.

A bar bell is the usual adornment although metal discs and studs fashioned from ivory or bone are also used in tribal societies, where it is often performed to mark the passage of an adolescent to manhood. As with the Prince Albert, the piercing can be stretched and bars of increasing size can be placed and hung with larger and larger studs. This will widen the head of the penis considerably, some comparing the feeling to that of a steel dildo. For stretching procedures, which can be painful, some recommend the use of desensitising sprays often sold in sex shops to delay orgasm.

Some piercers need to know the circumference of the erect penis to gauge how long the ampallang should be, which can be an uncomfortable process. I was once asked to go and measure the width of my erection with a set of callipers. Trying to coax life into stubborn equipment on a cold Winter's day in the often rudimentary toilets of the average piercing parlour is not conducive to male sexual response. It may be a wise decision to measure your width beforehand, or find someone who does not use this method.

Foreskins can be pierced for decorative effect and some benefit can be obtained by studs rubbing up against the shaft of the erect penis. Slave owners often did this in ancient Rome to keep slaves chaste ('infibulation') and the labia can also be pierced and locked. It is far from unknown for self-defined 'slaves' to continue this practice today, of their own free will.

The apadravya is a vertical piercing, either through the shaft or the glans, much rarer than the aforementioned devices although it has its devotees. The frenum is a piercing of the loose skin beneath the head of the penis. In conjunction with other piercings this can be used to prevent erection in the context of bondage and submission games, a ring being flipped over the flesh of the penis from the original piercing. Heavy rings placed through several piercings can also be secured by means of padlocks.

The guiche is a ring inserted in the flesh between the scrotum and the anus, the insertion of which is sometimes an undignified process. This is very common around the South Pacific where a rawhide thong is used. In the West it is customary to use rings or a barbell although some prefer to have fabric through the aperture. This is a difficult piercing to heal and it is worth considering whether you have the patience to endure a considerable amount of discomfort. Many guiches grow out, mine did twice – this is a common experience where flat parts of the body are pierced.

It is also possible to insert a ring above the penis if you have shaved your pubic hair. This placing can be sore for a month or so but eventually there is the possibility of clitoral stimulation during intercourse when the female is on top. The sensation of having a ridge of flesh where none was present formerly can be pleasurable to both men and women.

The Hafada is particularly popular in the Arab world where it is seen as a rite of passage into adult life. The piercing is at the base of the penis on the scrotal sac. It enables the scrotum to e stretched to a much greater extent than previously. One popular practice is to attach a weight to the ring which will provide pleasant stimulation during activity on all fours as it swings back and forth.

Navels have been pierced for decorative reasons in a variety of world cultures and although it has no direct erotic stimulus, anything

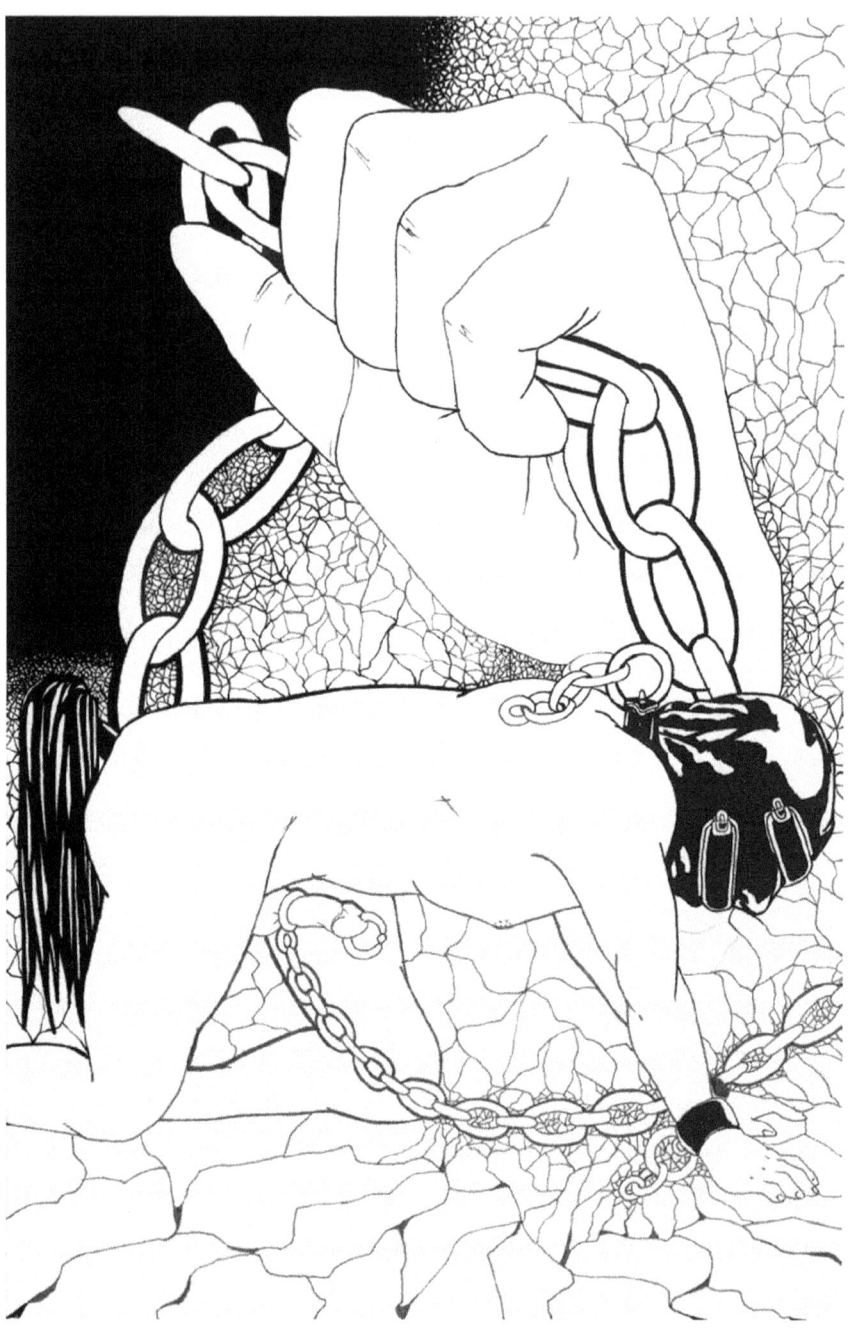

that contributes to the well being of the wearer can be said to be erotic in a wider sense. These piercings can be extremely troublesome and require great care on the part of the wearer who would be well advised to abandon jeans or any other form of rough material which will irritate the piercing during the healing process. Fresh air and salt water will help most of all but sometimes these piercings just don't take and one is forced to abandon the process.

Many of these male genital piercings stimulate parts of the vagina that are usually ignored during intercourse with an unpierced partner. It has been defined as being "fucked and fingered" simultaneously. For this reason alone, embarking on a series of piercings is a way of keeping sex in a long term relationship vibrant and exciting.

Nipple piercings are becoming more common now on men and women but they are the hardest piercing to look after, along with the navel. They can be troublesome as they heal, especially female nipples, due to the milk ducts. Another problem is allergies to various metals or even to cleaning solutions used. For this reason salt water is the best cleansing solution. The healing time is about two months, less for a man. They may occasionally ooze pus during this period but the majority of piercings heal successfully. Women often have the feeling that their nipples are permanently erect after piercing and the size and shape of the nipples are often enhanced.

Rotating rings on any piercing is a pleasurable activity, whether in an erotic situation or not. Nipple piercings can be pulled or twisted to great effect, although this must take place after the healing process. Stretched nipple piercings are particularly eye catching, especially when the process has resulted in dramatically enlarged nipples.

Opinion is divided as to the erotic benefits of piercing male nipples, some deriving great pleasure and some feeling very little. Whatever the results there is also the psychological effects to be considered, particularly their use during role play. Some submissives may treasure them as a sign of servitude or bondage to their superiors. At one time, which nipple was pierced was a sign that the wearer was submissive or dominant; dominants were, in any case, rarely pierced or adorned, but these ideas seem now to have been abandoned.

Many authorities are agreed that it is possible to increase feminine response considerably by piercing the clitoral hood. Although some can be place horizontally, clitoris hoods are usually pierced vertically, the vertical piercing provides more stimulation. One of the barbells holding the vertical piercings in place is usually visible while the bar holding the balls rests across the clitoris. Healing should be completed within two weeks and careful manual stimulation can commence during this period. A further advantage to this piercing is, as an ex partner of mine, Glamorpussy, said, "At least they know where it is now!" This procedure is dangerous and must only be done by an expert. The results may vary from extreme sensitivity to deadening of response which is the last thing anyone wants. Having discussed the piercings which have a direct sexual effect it remains only to say that piercing is often a rite of passage for the individual, in the same way that tattooing, branding or scarification (cutting the flesh), can be. At the very least the individual is asserting control over his or her own body. Lovers may also form a stronger bond by having similar piercings at the same time.

Labial rings are mostly decorative and can be worn as a tribute to certain partners; they should heal within two weeks. Probably the first time most people became familiar with this practice was after reading The Story Of O in which the willing eponymous slave allows her labia to be pierced and rings to be inserted.

There is apparently not much sensation to be gained from wearing rings in the outer labia although with several rings in place there will be stimulation of the shaft of the penis as it enters and leaves the vagina. Piercing the inner labia does provide an increase in pleasurable sensation and many people do get pleasure from hanging weights from labial rings, a favourite activity being dancing without underwear. The use of vibrators with genital piercings gives a great deal of pleasure to many and it is also possible to attach chains to rings through a variety of piercings to create a complex erotic sensation.

Other extreme forms of body modification include splitting the shaft of the penis in two which has been practised by Australian aborigines in tribute to a lizard with a split penis. Sexual function can continue after this operation but there are documented cases where it hasn't.

Japanese gangsters have been known to make an incision in the penis and insert a pearl to commemorate each year of their life in prison. After bandaging the wound, there is a growth similar to a wart. Roughly the same effect (for the female) can be achieved a lot less painfully by wearing heavily ridged condoms.

Another technique for increasing sensitivity in the genitals is shaving. It is important to use a good quality safety razor and use moisturiser afterwards as skin tends to develop spots and rashes but this area soon becomes accustomed to being shaved. Apart from the visual effect, the tactile sensation of stroking or kissing smoothly shaved skin has to be experienced to be believed. Splashing cold water over yourself when the process is completed will close the pores of the skin and also build up sex energy. Quite why Victorian authorities thought that cold baths were an antidote to supposedly sinful sexuality remains a mystery – the opposite is true. Many Tantrics recommend daily immersion of the genitals in cold water for a certain period of time; you must experiment to find what works best for you but there is no doubt that cold water works wonders, even if it takes courage to take the plunge at first.

Further advantages to shaving or depilation is that it opens up more areas for body play such as the application of clothes pegs which tend to slip on body hair. Tattoos and scarifications are considerably more impressive than when hidden under a covering of hair. Come on, chaps, it's not the 1970s, shave it off. (You'll look bigger, too.)

Corsets

Although women in corsets have often featured in erotica created by men and for men, many women today feel empowered by clothing which accentuates their femininity. The recent revival of the corset as outerwear has enabled contemporary designers to use lurid colours and materials such as metal and fibre glass to create a futuristic style appropriate for the 21st century. This is a style light years away from the stereotypical image of the subjugated Victorian woman gasping for air inside her tightly laced corset, owing more the 'look but don't touch' body armour worn by some dominant women.

While the corset is currently fashionable, drawings found at Neolithic sites of women laced into animal skins date from 20,000 years ago. The Romans laced slaves into tight clothing and Catherine de Medici insisted that her ladies and maids reduced their waists to a circumference of thirteen inches. This measurement means little to most people but the corset fetishist would be (appropriately) swooning at the thought of a thirteen inch waist. Any writing on the subject by devotees is likely to fetishise the circumference of the waist. Nineteen inches! Eighteen inches! Tighter, ever tighter…

In the mid 20th century Ethel Granger became a legend among body modification enthusiasts because of her thirteen inch waist, reduced from twenty-three inches. Encouraged by her husband, who also fetishised high heels and piercing, she maintained a tight lacing regime for more than 50 years, her thirteen inch waist being immortalised in the Guinness Book Of Records as the worlds smallest waist. This extreme waist reduction requires fanatical dedication but is by no means unusual. Many develop the taste for confinement and soon find that they feel unsatisfied without the corset's tight embrace.

Terence Sellers, author of The Correct Sadist, a professional New York dominatrix and therapist, is of the opinion that corsetry is a fetish for numbers and measurements. (A mania for numbers and lists is a feature of the Marquis de Sade's writing.) Just as some corporal punishment enthusiasts devise endless lists of penalties for various misdemeanours – detailing the number of strokes obsessively – a seventeen or sixteen inch waist measurement becomes in itself exciting. That said, the great majority of corset enthusiasts are excited by the way corsets emphasise the curves of feminine breasts and buttocks, and also by undertones of bondage and s/m activity. At one time I could close a 22 inch corset but this was when I was on the E plan diet, (regular clubbing and ecstasy,) remember folks, this magical love inducing substance was invented as a diet suppressant, so use it!

Fakir Musafa, the American Body Art pioneer, divides corset enthusiasts into three categories:

those who wish to shape the body; those, often transvestites, who wish to identify with women and an ideal of femininity by wearing their clothing; and those who seek erotic discomfort. Fakir Musafa once reduced his own waist from twenty-nine inches to nineteen, one of his many body modification experiments which owe something to tribal cultures and much to his own courage and ingenuity. Film stars such as Jean Harlow may have removed a rib to improve their figure but Fakir Musafa's impressive results prove that drastic waist reduction is possible without surgery.

Corsets are in use by male fetishists for a variety of reasons although they are mostly popular with transvestites who wish to acquire a more feminine figure by their use. Unfortunately, many cross dressers forget that large hands, bulging Adam's apples and the gangling gait of a six foot tall man are not immediately reminiscent of the femininity they wish to emulate. There are also men who wish to experience the tight constricting embrace of a corset purely for sensual reasons. Fakir Musafa recommends making love while both partners are corseted: '...all your internal organs and your sexual components are in different positions, with different tensions.'

Until the recent proliferation of material on fetishism and s/m, most information on corsets in a sexual context came from the Victorian era, often in magazine correspondence which was usually fictional. Common themes include the disciplining of unruly maids or schoolgirls by enforced tight lacing, dominant women cross-dressing submissive men, and the ritual of attaching a woman by her upraised hands to a corset rail so that a number of maids could tighten stays to the utmost. Contemporary writing stresses the myriad possibilities of role play, often hymning the praises of dominant women in corsets which naturally enhance feminine curves.

There follows a summary of some of the many current uses of the corset in sex play. Black leather corsets are particularly appropriate for dominant women who may find that their use enhances the appropriate upright and aloof posture. Such a garment may also be a subliminal reminder that the submissive will have no access to the body of the dominant. Incompetent lacing of the dominant's corset can be used as an excuse for punishment, not that dominants often have to wrack their brains for reasons to punish anyone. Tighter lacing of the submissive's corset is a potent threat.

Submissives may feel an extra thrill from wearing their corset in work social situations. Assuming that the submissive has not been laced so tight that any sort of movement is painful, friends and colleagues will remain unaware what lurks beneath the socially acceptable outerwear – a similar clandestine pleasure to that experienced by wearers of genital jewellery and other exotic piercings.

Long laces can be used in the manner of a whip or a crop and also to tie the submissive's hands to their sides or to attach them to a particular location. These laces can also be used in preference to a collar and leash as a means of leading the wearer around. Full length corseting after corporal punishment will also prevent the submissive from easing the sting by rubbing thrashed buttocks by preventing access to this hot flesh. Particularly demonic dominants may wish to put itching powder on the inside of the corsets. Slaves can be secured to the floor or walls of a dungeon, or indeed anywhere else, by means of padlocks attached to rings mounted on the corset. Romantics may find heart shaped padlocks add a welcome light touch to dark and doomy dungeon etiquette. This is supposed to be *fun*. But if you'd rather be miserable please yourselves...

In a fashion context, the first world war seemed to have brought the era of the tiny waist to a close although correspondence on the subject continued in magazines such as London Life for decades afterwards. While fetishists have never forgotten the corset, it was not until Jean Paul Gaultier dressed Madonna in a cone cupped corset that mass media took notice of this enduring fashion once more. Since then, designers have competed to create colourful and outlandish designs.

Some basic definitions – basques and waspies may appear similar to corsets although neither garment reduces the waist. Corsets come in two halves, laced at the back and fastened at the front with a steel busk. Whale bone is no longer used in the lining; the spiral foundation is usually metal. Some specialists offer traditional designs in cotton and satin, while rubber and leather are currently popular.

First time buyers should remember that the ideal corset should be four inches smaller than your natural waist measurement. Corsets must be treated gently at first, as careless use will destroy the garment but common sense should tell when enough is enough.

With any luck, a corset should provoke the sort of love making that leaves one or both partners close to a swooning fit. In this case, the Victorian tradition of keeping smelling salts handy to revive those suffering from a fainting fit may still be valid. Although with more and more men experimenting with confinement and erotic discomfort, the prone figure in need of revival is increasingly likely to be a man.

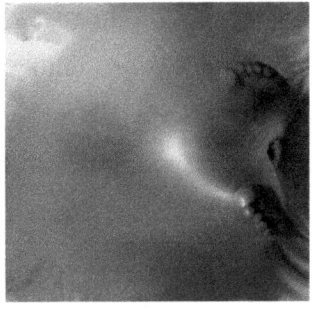

Rubber

The use of rubber in fashion is now so prevalent that there must be people who do not connect its use with sex at all. Rubber has become just one of many fetish styles that can be worn in clubs without identifying the wearer as a hardcore kinkster. Sexually, the appeal is easily enough explained. The feel of warm rubber moulded to the body provides a 'second skin' effect. Hence Skin Two, the best fetish magazine available. Many rubber enthusiasts enjoy the smell of the body's secretions mixed with the powerful odour of the material. In conjunction with the use of masks and bondage, the effect can be a loss of body outline. This can lead to the sort of weightless, timeless sensation which has much in common with out of body states sought by mystics and occultists. Other contexts in which rubber is often used include water sports, adult baby scenarios, sub/dom games, medical scenarios, full body enclosure or suspension.

Many of the more extreme procedures are complex and require expensive equipment. The use of masks and oxygen deprivation may trigger vivid hallucinations, a dangerous ecstasy sought by some, but breath play, particularly auto erotic asphyxiation, is often lethal, as there's a two second window between ecstasy and death, and crunching on an orange full of speed didn't help one poor wretch. In any case there's easier ways to get a harder dick and a spacier fucked up high, various drugs do this without leaving your loved ones left to grieve forever. To return to the use of rubber in a more innocuous fashion context, beginners should know that rubber needs to be sprayed with silicone spray to get the gleam which most people desire. A recent development is liquid latex which can be sprayed direct from the can onto the skin. Glitter can be added to create effects which suit club lighting.

Sex Accessories

The cock strap is a useful device for prolonging an erection indefinitely. This is a leather strap (originally camel hide) which wraps around the scrotum and penis. When pulled tight this will keep the blood in an erection and allow greater pleasure and yet simultaneously delay an orgasm, ideal conditions for the Tantric practice of Karezza (prolonged intercourse without orgasm). If you are using a home made device, wrap the strap once around your genitals then, having crossed it over above the penis, loop it downwards, dividing your testicles in two. Wrap around the scrotum once more, forming a figure of eight and then finally tie the device above the penis. It should not be too tight but only you can be the judge of the most effective pressure. Practice makes perfect.

And there's worse hobbies. These devices can be bought from sex shops, through mail order catalogues or can be made from shoe laces, stockings, elastic bands or even rolled out condoms. The only danger from this device is if you are stupid enough to use it while exhausted or intoxicated and fall asleep with it on. In which case, if you're unable to free it yourself, an extremely painful and embarrassing visit to the casualty department of your local hospital may ensue.

Similarly cock rings may be used to stretch the scrotum and keep the penis perpetually half erect. There are some dangers to the use of these items but common sense (and self preservation) should tell you to be careful where the sensitive testicles are involved.

The safest way to experience heightened pleasure is by using an elastic band although some metal cock rings can be opened like handcuffs and are much safer to use. If using a solid cock ring you will have to fit your testicles through the opening then the rest of the genitalia. With the right size ring there should be a bigger, firmer erection than normal and it is possible to continue making love after orgasm, given a pause so that the glans is not too sensitive to continue. Getting the right aperture is critical here. Too small is painful but too big means that the blood will not be trapped in the penis and the erection will not be sufficiently enhanced. These rings can be worn throughout the day, giving the wearer the sensation of perpetual tumescence.

Ball weights or scrotum stretching collars have been worn in tribal cultures to permanently stretch the scrotum but they can also be worn for a temporary thrill. The sensation has been described as if someone is fellating the testicles and the pleasures of self love are greatly enhanced by the wearing of these items.

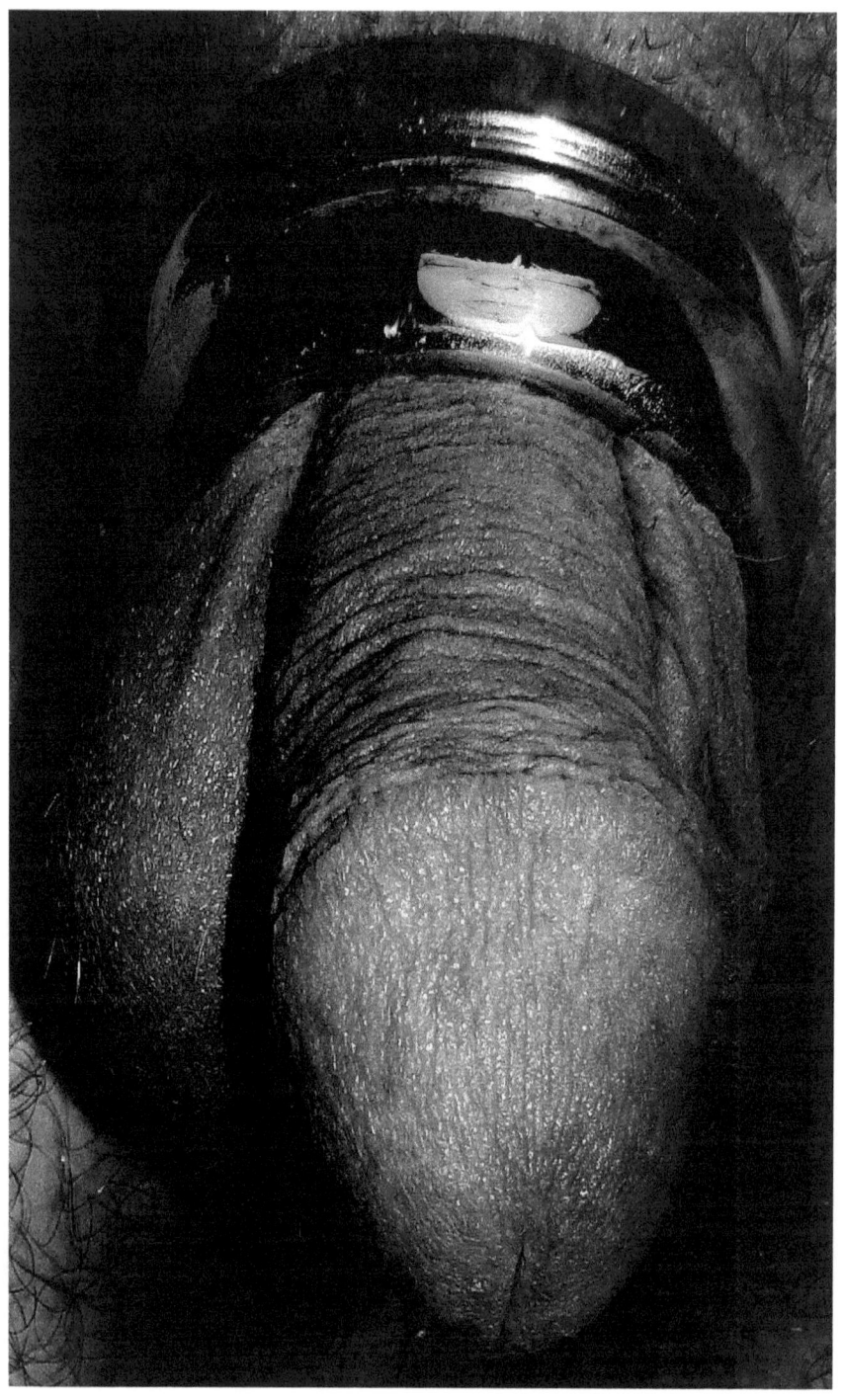

Bisexuality

Bisexuality may not seem very radical these days but there are still more men living this lifestyle than admitting to do so. Some entertainers and artists may be allowed to live outside the rigid categories that most people still cling to but most men and women identifying as bisexual can expect to be criticised by both hetero- and homosexuals. They will find few of their own persuasion among whom to seek unity and strength. Most heterosexuals and a large proportion of homosexuals believe that anyone attempting to identify themselves as bisexual are if fact gay but too scared to admit it.

When I recently commented that a well known actor was bisexual, an otherwise liberal woman became vehement in her opposition to this hardly controversial comment. "He's gay." She said. "He sleeps with men and women." I replied. "Then he's gay!" she insisted, at a volume which enabled everyone in the room to hear this ignorant assertion. It is depressing how often such comments can be heard even in London, that traditional haven for those who would practise alternative lifestyles.

The situation is complicated by the number of bisexuals who refuse to identify as such. There are large numbers of gay men who have sex with women on occasion but would never identify themselves as bisexual. These same men will probably have had sex with men who identify themselves as straight. Some people say bisexuality is 'the best of both worlds' but it often appears to be the worst, at least in terms of media or public acceptability. As the immortal Bernard Manning said, "Bisexual? I'd hate to be rejected by both sexes."

Meanwhile the sexuality itself will not be denied, although it sometimes finds expression in complex displacement behaviour. A number of dominatrices have commented on the men who come to

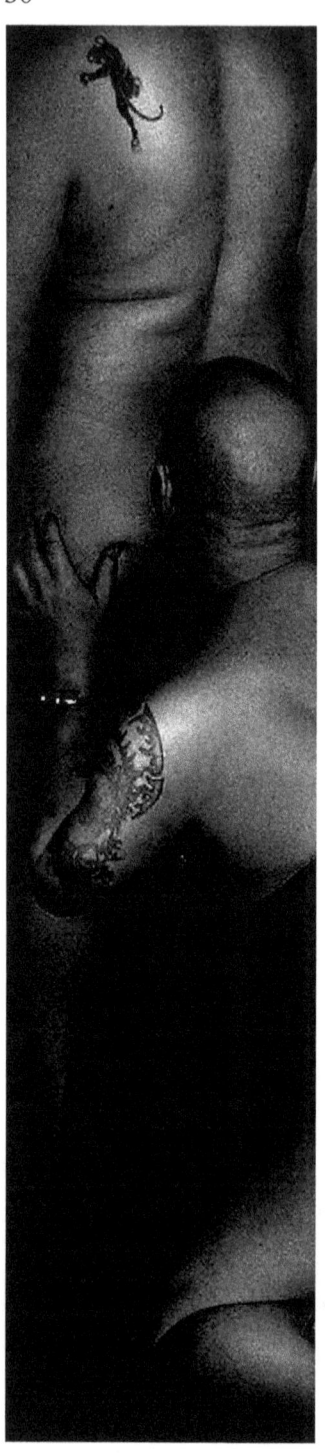

them to experience 'enforced homosexuality'. New York dominatrix and author Terence Sellers has coined the term 'encrypted homosexual' for the type of man who pays sex workers to order him to perform various homosexual acts. These might include dressing up as a woman, being humiliated in ways which include anal sex with various objects or being 'made to' submit to a man. In this case the presence of the dominatrix somehow legitimises the homosexual act he cannot bring himself to experience otherwise, although it is obviously a strong drive. This is one of the times when the often overused comment 'he's in denial' has some validity.

Truman Capote encapsulated this state of mind decades ago in Breakfast At Tiffany's. Holly Golightly is using the word diapers metaphorically here as she describes one of her men '…he had a stinking childhood.' 'If it was so stinking why does he cling to it?' 'Use your head. Can't you see that Rusty feels safer in diapers than he would in a skirt? Which is really the choice, only he's awfully touchy about it. He tried to stab me with a butter knife because I told him to grow up and face the issue, settle down with a nice fatherly truck driver.'

One of the reasons bisexuality remains such a secret is that it's rarely portrayed in the mass media, or is only seen in material intended for a gay audience. Although there has been a recent media avalanche of sex and depravity, there remains a peculiar taboo against straight looking men enjoying each other for the delectation of women consumers. While it is acceptable for men to consume 'lesbian' erotica, as long as the participants look nothing like most lesbians, women find it very hard to find material about straight looking men playing with each other. I use straight here in the sense of not having gym honed muscles, not being particularly photogenic or possessing exaggerated masculine signifiers for the purpose of gay fetishism – in other words, blokes who look as ragged and unstyled as your average husband.

Although some women so want these acts portrayed, mainstream sex publishers will not satisfy this demand. Perhaps the men in charge of the industry fear a further erosion of male dignity if ordinary women were to be exposed to ordinary men engaged in sex play with each other. This should be rectified. There's a gap in the market entrepreneurs.

At a time when marketing directly to individuals or categories of people is of paramount importance it is likely that bisexuals will remain in the shadows. There just aren't enough people identified as bisexual to make it worth targeting them with goods and services and the pink pound has blown bisexuality out of the water. This doesn't make the number of married men cruising for casual sex with men any less but they will never have the visibility or the unity and strength of the gay community. It seems odd at a time when two parent households are a minority that every political party that has a chance of winning any elections still insists that marriage is the best possible lifestyle. Gays and bisexuals have votes too, but for the moment it appears that one must be a married Christian to be taken seriously as a potential leader in Britain and America. Utterly ridiculous.

The taboo is puzzling as it is hardly unknown for men in early adolescence to experience same sex interplay and situational homosexuality in prisons is well known. Then at some point it becomes untenable for these same people to repeat the experiment. Perhaps the whole situation is best summed up by a gag which many gay men know encapsulates a useful nugget of truth. 'What's the difference between a straight guy and a bisexual?' 'Eight pints of lager.'

Footnote

"Many men desire to know the pleasures of homosexual sex and a re forced to suppress this desire because of the social stigma that still, in the year 1997, attaches to being overtly homosexual. Compelled by convention to maintain the heterosexual charade, we see how their desire to be with a man is controlled, overshadowed by the woman they must deal with. If he is fortunate, that woman may require him to make love to a man. The woman will then 'make him into' a homosexual – by rejecting him for sex; by initiating him into gay sex; by feminising him; by 'allowing' him to do whatever he wants to do with a man." *Terence Sellers, Dungeon Evidence*

Switching

Just as the terms gay, heterosexual and bisexual ignore the shifting sands of human sexuality, perhaps it is time to say that the terms sub, dom and switch (alternatively sub and dom) are reductive and constricting. These terms also confer status, something which sometimes causes friction of the wrong sort whenever scene players get together.

In an ideal world the status of sub and dom scene players should be equal but this is far from the case in practice. The behaviour of some self hating male subs might explain why. Although women often find it refreshing to be in a position of power they can still recoil at the sight of a nude man crawling round on the floor begging to be abused by total strangers. Often these men have been bottling up their desires for years and their first attempts at social interaction are about as graceful as a drunken sailor on shore leave. They have little or no interest in the personality of the woman they are intent on submitting to, they are just seeking a potential provider of a particular service.

Subs tend to turn up with an endless list of demands. Submissives tend to be very 'toppy', to use the scene jargon. I've lost count of the times I have heard subs whining on about the poor service they are getting from their dominants. It is far from unknown to see supposed submissives twisting their torso round so they can see exactly where the lashes are landing and complaining about the angle of trajectory and the speed and you don't to use one of those, you want to get a proper crop, put more wrist into it, not that much wrist, try and stand further forward so the cane strikes both cheeks equally, harder! Softer! Look, this just isn't working…

The idea that some tops might get their pleasure regardless of

what is happening to their partners or precisely because it is painful or frustrating for them seems to have got lost somewhere along the way. The mindset was summed up perfectly in Fetish Times Editor Spencer Woodcock's cartoon of a stroppy looking slave berating a bemused looking dom with the words 'I may be your slave but you're not going to boss me about.'

There are also masochists who wish for nothing more than a therapeutic flogging and tire of dom players who insist on a long drawn out pantomime before it can begin. 'I'm a masochist but NOT submissive' is often worth saying, if you wish to stand your ground. You'll need to be firm because there are plenty of dominants who refuse to accept any view which disputes the concept of their own divinity. It seems obvious to state that dominant men and women are no better than their supposedly inferior submissive partners but there are plenty of tops who have confused their play persona with consensus reality. This confusion is a fairly obvious source of friction socially, once the party is over. Similar confusion occurs on the occult scene when someone chosen to embody a certain god or goddess remains convinced of their divinity long after it is time to get the drinks in. Scene veteran Ishmael Skyes has identified the condition as Dominatrix Toxaemia.

Top's disease is better. While there is hardly a shortage of experienced dominant women, both professionals and enthusiastic amateurs, men who can act out the dominant role with style and panache are few and far between. Some project a harsh and aggressive persona that sometimes begs the question whether they are comfortable in this role or are merely still angry at some unresolved childhood trauma.

Many men would rather hide their submissive side than risk being 'demoted' to submissive. Those men keen to assert that they are only dominant are protesting too much, in a similar manner to homophobic males who loudly protest their heterosexuality. Submissive females often say that genuinely dominant males who are comfortable with this polarity are few and far between. It takes courage to admit to a submissive side or even to admit to being a switch, when this is surely the most natural choice of all.

The perceptive fetish writer and scene personality Peter Birch once summed up the situation thus: "A party of dominants is like the staff of a South American army, lots of fancily dressed colonels giving each other orders and no-one taking an notice. A party of submissives is like a crowded tea party in a British vicarage, lots of people bumping into each other and apologising profusely. A party of switches is an orgy, and that's where I want to be."

Shakespeare And Radical Desire

Alongside a great number of war re-enactors and history obsessives, the fetish scene contains many Shakespeare enthusiasts. Maybe it's the leather jerkins or the codpieces, or just that the bard attracts frustrated actors and other poseurs – a species not unknown in fetish clubs. The situation is the same in America. 'The Renaissance Faire here in Northern California is practically a slut's trade conference,' according to Dossie Easton and Catherine A. Liszt, the authors of the Ethical Slut – a wonderful handbook for anyone who wishes to attempt a polyamorous lifestyle. Easton and Liszt recommend that anyone seeking partners interested in radical sex should join a historical re-enactment group or visit a science fiction conference. The Dark Ages Society in England also contains those whose enthusiasm for dressing up and sub/dom role-play far exceeds that which you might expect to find in historical scholars. This is just one of the many historical societies which offer frequent opportunities for the wearing of leather, the administration of sound scourgings by the light of the moon and the consumption of copious amounts of alcohol, often in horn-shaped receptacles.

Aside from the dressing-up and the showing off there are other aspects to Shakespeare's work that will commend themselves to those who identify themselves as perverts. Anthony and Cleopatra contains a line which is often quoted to illustrate that it is not only sado-masochists who enjoy the intermingling of pain and pleasure: 'A lover's pinch which hurts and yet is desired.'

Gender confusion is often a theme in the plays. Part of the

Lady MacBeth.

entertainment for Shakespeare's audience would have been watching boys dressed as women masquerading as men. A line from the sonnets – 'she is the master-mistress of my soul'- encapsulates this sort of role play and also evokes domination and submission. Many of the sonnets seem to have been composed by someone who gets a thrill out of being cheated, ignored and generally abused, a state of mind familiar to submissive men and women, particularly sonnet 57 which depicts the narrator as slave. Those who are accustomed to being tied, teased and tormented will have experienced this bitter sweet joy many times – an ecstasy that builds to a passionate intensity far greater than that available to those who have easier access to their heart's desire. It may be sacrilege to suggest that we may have had far fewer than 154 sonnets if Shakespeare had had his fill of either his objects of desire but then he did not write at this length about his wife. Most of those who have been slaves to radical desire would agree that, very often, darkness is more attractive than the light.

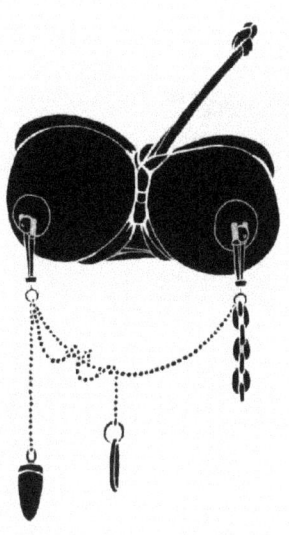

The Dark Side Of Tantric Sex

"Sexuality, even at its most perverse is implicitly religious. Sex is the ritual link between man and nature." *Camille Paglia*

Tantric sex has recently been presented in the media as a form of sexual yoga, a harmless diversion for couples to practice while listening to their whale song CDs by the light of aromatic candles. This is to ignore the deeper, darker tradition which can be more rewarding, for those with the courage to face up to their own demons. But even the sanitised version of Tantric sex presently on offer has much to recommend it. The best known technique to people who may have seen the coffee table book on the subject is prolonged sexual intercourse during which the male delays orgasm as long as possible in order to absorb the sexual energy generated by the female. Staring into a partner's eyes is a typical Tantric technique to delay male orgasm. As well as helping both partners bond together it is also possible to set the goal of concentrating upon whatever mystic symbols that both partners find appropriate or an affirmation of a mutual goal. Some Tantric practitioners believe that men absorb the fluids secreted during the female orgasm. The aim is to be in perpetual union with the Goddess, an aim that many men identifying as submissive can identify with. Veneration of the female principle through prolonged sexual union of male and female is the central tenet of this belief system as expressed by the well known mantra 'om mani padme hum', also known as the jewel in the lotus or, more prosaically, the penis in the vagina. In pagan ceremonies this is symbolised by the high priest or priestess dipping a dagger (the penis) into a chalice (vagina).

In theory, whatever sex energy is raised by prolonged orgasmless intercourse should rise upwards through the different chakras or energy centres and then flower in the highest chakra in the form of divine wisdom. (Some readers may be familiar with the seven chakra system popularised by Western occultists but this is not the only chakra system used in India.) Prolonged cunnilingus, particularly in the sixty-nine position, is an important rite as is the practice of male orgasm without the release of sperm. The 'full body' orgasm for men is easy to learn – a stronger, longer lasting orgasm that can be attained by using the muscle which blocks off the flow of urine to prevent the emission of sperm. Although this requires practice the exercise can be done anywhere and will also increase the potential strength and duration of the erection. Women will also benefit from these techniques which aim to lengthen the time of any sexual encounter considerably and in which they are not mere accessories for men to use for their own pleasure. The Western version of Tantric sex has become known as Sex Magick and was originally popularised by occultists (who persist on spelling magic with a concluding k to differentiate their form of magic from that of stage magicians). Along with astrology, yoga, hypnotism and certain other alternative health treatments, this was once stigmatised as 'black magic'. Sex Magick is in fact nothing more than a form of sexual meditation. Just as repeating a word or phrase helps to establish a trance during meditation, it is possible to motivate yourself to greater achievement by concentrating on what you wish for during sexual activity. This is similar to repeating an affirmation until it sinks into your sub-conscious, a kind of self hypnosis.

Valuable as all the above ideas are there is a much more powerful variant of Tantric Sex, dubbed by some the left hand path, much of

which is based on smashing taboos. This involves facing up to whatever revolts you sexually and deliberately indulging in it, an important technique for breaking down entrenched habits, indeed dismantling an entire personality. Even if the person who emerges from this process appears strikingly similar to the old, he or she is likely to have their feet just a little bit off the ground. (The terms right and left hand path derive from the occult. Right hand path occultists tend to be either self styled white witches or middle class men bonding together on drum banging weekends – beards are de rigueur as are the singing of folk songs. Many regard the sight of an inverted pentacle as proof positive that the cloven footed one is among us, forgetting that 'the devil' is a Christian corruption of nature gods such as Pan and The Green Man. The left hand path denotes a willingness to explore the darker side, to conquer our inner demons by facing them, whatever this might cost.)

Incidentally, it is not necessary to abandon rational thought to enjoy the benefits of mysticism, it can be used as and when necessary. Most sex magick practitioners perform a banishing ceremony before and after each ritual and then return to everyday consciousness to continue with their more mundane activities. Many fetishist activities could, of course, be said to be rituals in themselves. Enhancing these ritual aspects of fetishism requires only a defined space where these activities can take place – a 'chamber' either real or imagined. Most of these rituals start with a purification, the ceremony itself follows then a ritual banishment of whatever energy has been raised. The purification could be anything from deep breathing and visualisation to prolonged drumming, whipping, dancing till exhaustion, drug use etc. The work itself should be defined beforehand and the participants should proceed together towards an agreed goal. These three steps apply equally to a Bacchanalian orgy as to a solitary practitioner.

Initiation into many sects practising what the general public understands as witchcraft often involves being tied up, ritual scourging and the sort of group sex activities one is unlikely to encounter in present day Church of England. (Although who can say what the Church may resort to in their increasingly desperate attempts to get someone, anyone, to show up.) Some of these 'traditions' were invented comparatively recently but there certainly seems to be enough consumer demand to carry on regardless. It must be stressed that those working in this area are seeking to alter their own thought processes and strengthen their sexual appetites rather than conjuring up supernatural beings. We should all be aware by now that these 'angels and demons' reside inside ourselves and, even if they do manifest with chemical assistance or by pushing ourselves through extremes of pain or exhaustion, they are still figments of our imagination.

Left hand path Tantra certainly does not exclude homosexuality or any other supposedly 'deviant' sexuality; seekers after enlightenment are even encouraged to embrace what they usually find to be so repugnant. (It should go without saying that I am referring to adult consensual sexuality here.) There is also a genuine centuries old tradition of Norse occultists who have used cross dressing and gay sexuality to cast spells and send out astral being to do their will. Effeminate behaviour and passive anal intercourse was seen as unmanly and shameful at a time when men were expected to be fearless warriors but nearly all occult paths eventually involve bisexuality in theory and practice, if only to confront what one may be afraid of. Assuming the opposite sexuality to that which one is used to involved the dissolution of personality, an important taboo busting exercise. Virginia Woolf was referring to the magic of words when she stated 'One must be woman-manly or man-womanly' but the principle holds true for anyone seeking to explore

what it really means to be human. Those defining themselves as either dominant or submissive should also be capable of seeing how the other half lives occasionally. At the very least, these Tantric techniques can increase one's capacity for and enjoyment of sex. It can also be a richly rewarding path to follow. But perhaps the most valuable work one can do is to face those areas of one's sexuality which have become blocked for reasons of guilt, society's disapproval, or denial of one's own basic drivers.

A modern day adept need not go as far as the dissident Tantric mystics who copulated with corpses, indeed they absolutely shouldn't, (for the literal minded bores, many of whom will no doubt be complaining about this book as soon as it's published). These dissidents bathed in ashes from crematoriums and ate their own excrement (not likely to be seen in Tantric sex coffee table books for some time yet). Still, the true Tantric path, involves exploring the dark side of our sexuality, the highs and lows, the very limits of what humans are capable.

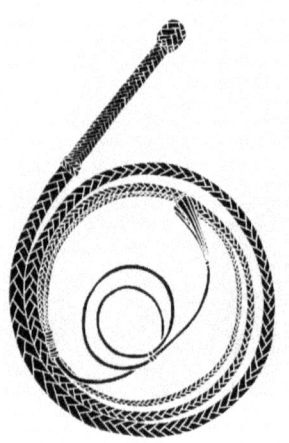

Fetish Sex Work

"Respectable writing about prostitution was still of the 'road to ruin' variety, emphasizing destitution, exploitation and the white slave traffic, and ignoring the prosperous and relatively easy lives many prostitutes appear to have led."

This quote from Stephen Inwood's history of London refers to the 1930s but may as well refer to the contemporary media which relays endless disinformation about sex work. Why is it so very rare for there to be a positive portrayal of prostitution in the mass media? The term sex worker has been around for some decades now and is presently finding its way into mainstream use. It is a mystery why it has taken thousands of years to have a non judgemental term for a provider of these essential services. (There is also no positive word for a woman who enjoys sex while most of us can think of many derogatory expressions for the same condition. Only recently, a woman journalist in the Guardian referred to Monica Lewinsky as a 'slut'. Still, what would you expect from this puritan hair- shirted know it all student's favourite?)

We will probably have to wait for the decriminalisation of sex work for a less negative view. Perhaps when UK newspapers can sell advertising to sex workers we will finally see a positive portrayal of their age old trade.

Legalisation or effective de-criminalisation looks unlikely at the present but there is a precedent for state controlled prostitution in Britain, pioneered by the mediaeval church which accepted taxes from Southwark 'stewmongers' in the fourteenth century. In the fifteenth century the Bishop of Winchester issued ordinances which aimed to ban 'enticement', and the serving of food and drink. Women taking money

from customers were to 'ly still with them' through the night. Diseased, married and unwilling women were theoretically unable to work in these brothels.

This situation lasted until Henry VIII ordered the closure of the brothels in 1546. In practice this meant that commercial sex was relocated nearby, just as every time Westminster Council cracks down on unlicensed sex venues today it merely creates the same problem for adjoining boroughs.

(What follows was written in 1999 for the first edition of Radical Desire) "As more Islamic councillors get elected in areas like London's East End there will be an increasingly political struggle to eradicate the sex trade in the area. Already there is an initiative to evict sex workers from council premises in Tower Hamlets and they are keen to limit the burgeoning lapdancing trade." Why, it's Mystic Mark. I accurately predicted the current desperate situation where "No gays here" stickers disfigure Tower Hamlets. Better not say any more. What with opposition to 8th century theocratic idiocy being a tad dangerous. Although check my Martin Amis Jihad Rap on You Tube if you like. I've mixed his observations on male fear of female power among a certain religion. Despite some childish scrawl from a fat farting frump, who possesses no discernible skill or talent, and hates all men and most women, this track has been well received. In any case I have yet to be beheaded for this heretical dance track.

The fetish scene contains some sex workers who still enjoy sex enough to want to play with strangers and scene regulars. Some have spoken out to try to challenge the perception of sex workers as brutalised, drug addicted slaves in thrall to their vicious pimps. Unfortunately it's hard to compete with the endless tide of negative messages about sex which pour out from the media on a daily basis.

No television drama would be complete without scenes of pimps attacking their drug addicted whores. Yet fetish sex workers are often successful businesswomen and their personalities vary as widely as any other disparate collection of individuals. They are rarely victims as streetwalkers often are.

Although it is true that some street prostitutes may fall prey to violent pimps, this is not always the case. Just as some people with unconscious masochistic desires often engineer their own downfall, there are people in all walks of life who embrace failure rather than success. Those who wish to be victims will always find a way.

Perhaps the hardest thing about the business is hiding its existence from the neighbours or even the hall porter, should one have taken the sort of slightly upmarket flat that wealthy clients prefer to visit. There are occasional risks with unstable clients but then nurses and barmaids face the same problem of dealing with potentially violent men every single working day. At least sex workers can refuse to admit drunks.

Recently a sex worker and writer tried to get the negative media stereotype changed by giving an interview for a well known women's magazine. A journalist arrived at her house and place of work, interviewed her and her clients at length, promised copy approval, leaving her with the impression that this was to be a positive article. She felt close enough to her subject to share some detail about her cocaine addiction, which mummy and daddy had helped pay for, expensive cure and all. An extremely derogatory article finally appeared claiming that the journalist was poverty stricken but would never resort to such sleazy activities to make a living, unlike the hard hearted bitch she had interviewed.

Some might say that the sex worker was naïve to expect anything else from journalists, although this was a modern woman's magazine full of titillating articles about sex. It is still puzzling why sex workers

Sidonia Von Bork Very beautiful, highly intelligent,
THE best hardcore FemDom TheEnglishMansion.com

get such a bad press. Perhaps it's just the age old media practice of attacking competitors in the leisure industry. (And if more people were comfortable with their sexual appetites and their self image there might be less call for the dieting industry and fashion itself, which pays for the adverts which keeps the women's magazine industry afloat). It might be very different if the journalist in question had worked for a magazine that could legally take adverts for sex work.

There are a lot of people with vested interests in keeping sex dirty. Even as monogamous marriage appears to have utterly failed to keep patriarchy going, we are still told that marriage is a highly desirable way of keeping society in order. As sex workers are often the safety valve that allow many of these marriages to continue, perhaps they should be more valued than they presently are.

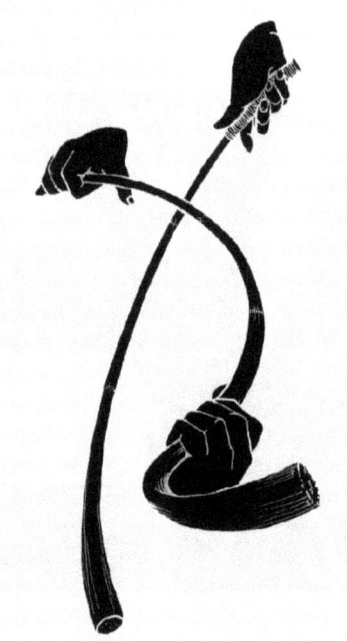

Radical Desire And Media Disinformation

"As yet the promiscuous cannot grow old gracefully. But this may say more about our ideas of dignity, than of aging."

Adam Phillips

Although we are bombarded with sexual images and ideas, most of the material is concerned with sex as a consumer activity. How many partners can we have? How many orgasms? Are we coming together? Does my partner look good enough to boast about? Will he/she enhance my status? The media treatment of sex often leaves one with the impression that the most radical form of sex takes place between old people, people who are not particularly photogenic (as defined by the advertising industry), and those who are over-weight. Men with bellies, women over forty: how dare these people have sex? How dare they exchange love and affection for no money? Why, the whole foundations of our society would tremble if guilt free sex was available outside of the confines of marriage.

This argument surfaces again and again on television and in the press, often by supposedly humorous writers. It's apparently very important that we keep on repeating the self hating message that only the photogenic are allowed to have sex.

Needless to say few of these journalists or filmmakers are particularly photogenic or possess gym honed bodies. It would be understandable if the people pouring scorn on over-weight men and middle aged women were fire and brimstone religious fundamentalists but these half smart media professionals see themselves as liberals.

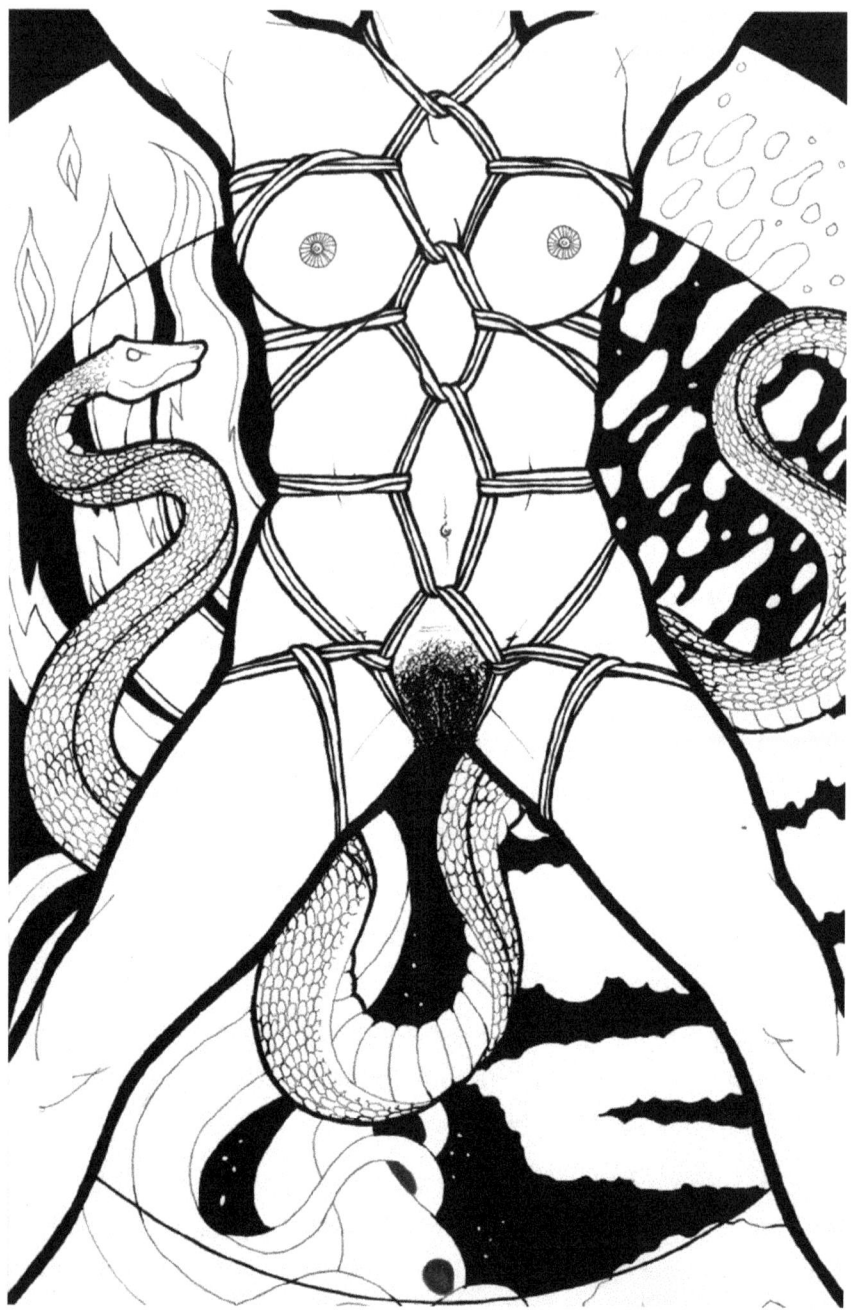

Perhaps it is simply that many columnists are paid to reflect the views of their readers and that toxic body consciousness has over taken us all.

Television is presently awash with cheap documentaries which aim to sneer at the sex scene while showing as much bare flesh as they can get away with. I have yet to see a sympathetic portrayal of the non commercial sex scene and I doubt if I ever will. Arthouse films are hardly any better. The documentary film maker Nick Broomfield made a film called 'Fetishes' set in a brothel in which he appeared satisfied with the portrait of himself as a grinning idiot steadfastly refusing to participate in any sexual activity or discuss his own tastes. He was, however, still interested enough to stand around getting in the way of a working house for a couple of weeks in order to demonstrate his own superiority to the sex workers and their clients. Dream on, Nick. You're not their superior, you're a berk with a camera using Fetishism to sell your work.

Respected literary writers are hardly any more open minded than tabloid journalists when it comes to sex. Martin Amis used to write about the "headache smell of pornography", referring to the odour of some glossy magazines. Not that this headache smell ever prevented him writing for, or making frequent appearances in men's magazines which are often thinly disguised soft-core pornography or doing interviews for Playboy etc.. The protagonist of Money, John Self, was deeply ashamed of his own need to masturbate, indeed of almost anything to do with sex. Even in a recent novel like Night Train, his characters are still dismissive of masturbation. This doesn't stop Amis trying to spice up his work with the inclusion of auto-erotic asphyxia, which he discovered at exactly the same time as his despised genre novelists. It remains unclear why an agnostic supposedly up with contemporary science is so keen to propagate a biblical taboo against self love.

It is also the case that most of the media is owned by conservatives who are well aware that the best way of controlling the masses is to limit their sexual options.

Larry Flynt, the publisher of Hustler magazine and a long time thorn in the side of the American legal system has been quoted as saying, "There is a widespread belief among many conservatives that if our sexual behaviour can be controlled, our whole lives can be bought into submission." Broadsheet newspapers are as guilty as any other in this respect.

Another of the many possible examples was the Guardian's obituary of Dominic Aury (the pseudonymous author of the Story of O). Her obituarist was careful to praise her more literary work while damning with faint praise The Story of O, a work which is surely destined for immortality. Dominic Aury, writing as Pauline Reage, wrote the book in the early fifties to entertain her lover, in order to keep their relationship going at a time when she feared the initial impetus was waning. In the process she created a literary novel in which dark sexuality is celebrated, particularly the submissive female. Among countless enthusiasts were Graham Greene, Harold Pinter, Brian Aldiss, J.G Ballard and jazz drummer Buddy Rich (who chose it as his book on his appearance on Desert Island Discs). Over half a century or so it has been both revered and reviled but the usual media stance is either that The Story of O is 'only' an erotic novel (as if that objective was easily enough accomplished, why not try to write one, you literary dickheads?) or that it is somehow a wicked attempt by men to subjugate women. Her male obituarist helpfully explained that it was a shame she had pandered to male fantasies. "That such a book, so clear in its perception of male fantasies, should

have been written by a women is strange enough. But it is stranger still that it should have been written by Dominic Aury, one of the most cultured, distinguished and measured minds of her generation." What. A. Dong.

Dominic Aury/Pauline Reage will of course be remembered long after this newspaper obituary but the patronising tone of the article is typical of the endless media campaign of disinformation about Kink, Radical Desire, call it what you will.

The one useful piece of information in the obituary was that O was first named Odile but then changed in order not to offend a friend of that name, ending some decades of philosophical speculation along the lines that O represents the character's search for oblivion or nothingness.

Most media treatments of Radical Desire ignore the obvious – these activities may look risible but they feel good. An obese, middle aged man squeezed into a rubber suit and hung upside down may not be an attractive image that can be used to sell some needlessly expensive and irrelevant product, but the point is that the individual inside the suit is communing with some of the most powerful sexual forces human beings can experience.

Given the media consensus that Kink is either sordid or dangerous, some think it's best to abandon the attempt to woo a mass audience. Perhaps these activities should only be enjoyed by those who are prepared to do without society's approval. This is to forget that gay campaigners have only won acceptance for their sexuality by decades of struggle and weathering the scorn and ridicule of the mainstream press. There is no reason why the full range of adult consensual sexuality shouldn't be as accepted as gay sexuality now is, if enough people have the courage to fight for it. It is certainly getting harder for the censors to control the general public who are by now all too familiar with the list of politicians and other pillars of conformity who are caught out indulging their perfectly natural desires for sex and drugs. This hasn't stopped a current member of the Conservative government retaining his position, (in Government, that is, not his position begging to be whipped by a black Dominatrix).

Although none of us are responsible for our sexual preferences we persist in feeling guilt when these are not 'appropriate' as defined by those who would sell us a lifestyle along with a received set of opinions. 'Deviant' sexuality remains a topic that is not easily discussed for fear of appearing sleazy or even 'evil'.

Pagans have propagated the credo 'an it harm none', that is to say, if something gives pleasure and does not harm other people it should be accepted. This is the majority view whatever the self appointed guardians of morality say.

The puritanical view may be propagated endlessly in mass market newspapers but there is plenty of evidence that the public do not always agree with it. The Daily Mail once had a picture of Madonna just after purchasing a strap on. The slogan was the usual hypocritical lies but the readers' comments were interesting: they were all in approval of Madonna. 'Lucky old Guy' or 'Go girl!' seemed to be the general consensus. (She was still married to Guy Ritchie at the time). It may be stating the obvious but let's remind the sex hating followers of St Paul, and the equivalent in other faiths, that the enjoyment of sexual activity is an entirely legitimate and life enhancing activity.

Scarification

Shortly before we were married, my first wife agreed to carve her initial into my chest, a bonding ritual that had absolutely nothing whatsoever to do with sexual pleasure. When the day came I wasn't sure whether she would want to use a scalpel to permanently scar my left pectoral but then, after seven and a half years of co-habitation most people could probably find it in themselves to shred the flesh of their loved ones. Housk Randall wanted to photograph the cutting in a way that would challenge the usual dark aesthetic associated with radical desire. The photography session went smoothly, perhaps too smoothly, for the relaxed atmosphere was not so conducive to extreme behaviour. It was a sunny afternoon in a quiet suburban street. Perhaps we should have been atop a hillside at midnight when the full moon was in Scorpio. Although I will never forget the incision and the vinegar and salt we rubbed in afterwards. At least we achieved something aesthetically pleasing without needing to ring for an ambulance. Whether this sort of light scarification will become de rigueur for modern married couples I can't say but surely it must be an option for those who want to move beyond having their names tattooed on each other. After our unfortunate and extremely painful divorce I eventually summoned up the courage to get Ruth Ramsden, my second and final wife, to carve an R over the D scarification. Whether I was out of practice or just older I don't know but it hurt like a Tabasco enema. Be that as it may, rubbing charcoal in completed the process and the scarification looks much better for the black tint. Boasting about this cutting edge (sorry) behaviour to Nina Hatchard, an intelligent women too busy for male preening, she brought me down to earth by saying, "like we used to do at school?" She meant no harm but this sacred skin sculpture isn't some crappy biro effort which needs covering, this is a Viking Warrior's Hard Runic Eternal Bond of...("Shut it, Granddad!").

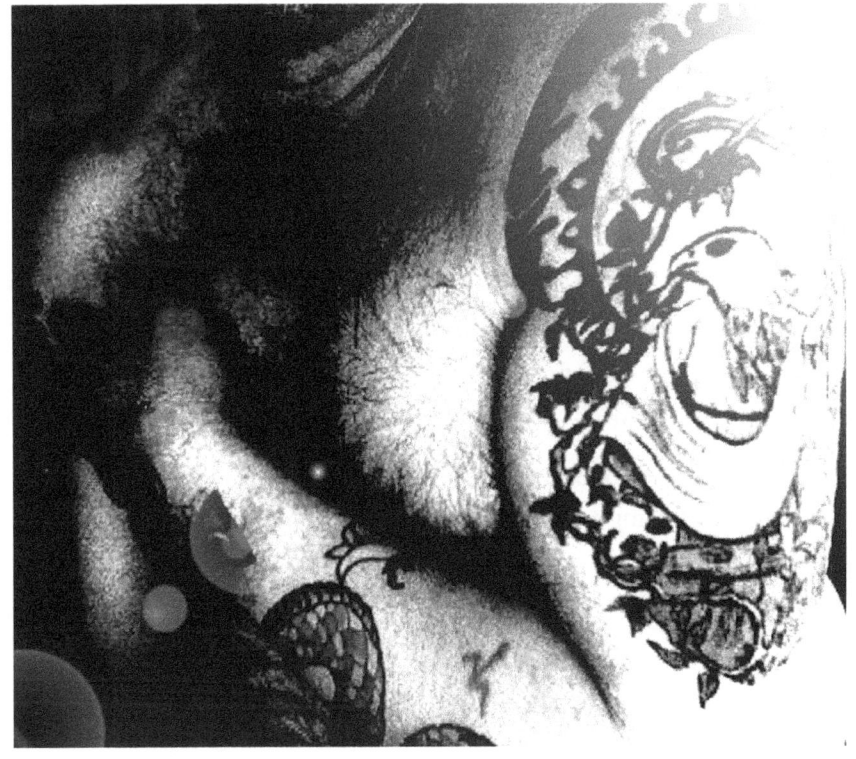

The Law Of Diminishing Returns

If there is a problem with the pursuit of sexual ecstasy it is that repetition very soon dulls the edge of whatever new high one might find. Human beings are programmed to repeat pleasurable activities, usually leading to greater consumption of whatever experience or substance is desired but it is important to remember that peak experiences are just that – they cannot be replicated or experienced as a regular hobby activity. Over-indulgence in anything blunts the edge of what used to be pleasurable. A member of the British Wildcat performance group who have suspended themselves from skewers in public has reported that the intensity of the experience lessens with each repetition. There is no reliable research into such extreme behaviour but the concept of tolerance is familiar to anyone who has ever used any addictive substance. Addiction is perhaps too prevalent in the media due to the marketing of various miracle cures and bogus therapies but it is still valid to state that radical desire can be addictive. Just as substance abusers realise that they need more and more of their preferred chemicals to get the same result, and eventually they need massive doses just to function normally, most kink enthusiasts get deeper and deeper into their obsession, pushing their bodies through greater pain barriers to intensify the altered states they desire. In the space of a few years I went from being repelled by the idea of piercing to exhibiting my Prince Albert and other genital piercings on television and in magazines literally making a dick of myself. Although some of this was to generate publicity for an obscure but innovative magazine, Fetish Times, and my first novel, my activities probably achieved little more than to reassure other men about their own possible shortcomings. There was a definite adrenalin buzz at first but like any other thrill, it didn't last. Soon I was bartering on-screen full frontal nudity on cable for a brief plug for that highly acclaimed first novel, The Dark Magus and The Sacred Whore. Yes, I'm now aware the title is too long, thank you. So I appeared on the Living Channel, exhibiting my pierced junk. "This is Mark who has written a murder mystery. Is it anything like Agatha Christie?" Well, however much we neo-noir novelists may try it's a hard gig trying to change the majority's perception of what a crime novel is. Just as persuading the public that kinksters are harmless may take some time.

Where desire becomes craving is a matter for individuals but it is usually necessary to take a break from whatever activity is being over indulged in order to regain its original power. Having said that, most people's journey through the undergrowth of their psyche usually involves a search for bigger and better highs, inevitably coming up against the law of diminishing returns. The simple answer to this is to vary the area of exploration, to find another option for a while and then to return to the original obsession refreshed and renewed.

What Trina Said

"Sir! Sir! What do you want sir?" The speaker was an attractive young blonde woman, an associate of a notorious Midlands occultist and club organiser. The said sorcerer was in the habit of reading my first novel to his slaves in bed at night. From this promising start the conversation roamed around a number of salacious topics. Some time later I needed to explain that I was presently experiencing some mental turbulence. As far as I knew I was maintaining well under the onslaught of some Ecstasy. But it was probably just as well to mention this, just to be on the safe side. "I'm in a very strange space at the moment, I said, intending

to explain about the chemical feel good factor. Yes, she said, mischievously, "It's your midlife crisis."

A joke which happened to be true. Still, at least this filthy strumpet has been spanked and thrashed often for her insolence. Although as she will have enjoyed every one of these impact play sessions the joke remains, as ever, on me.

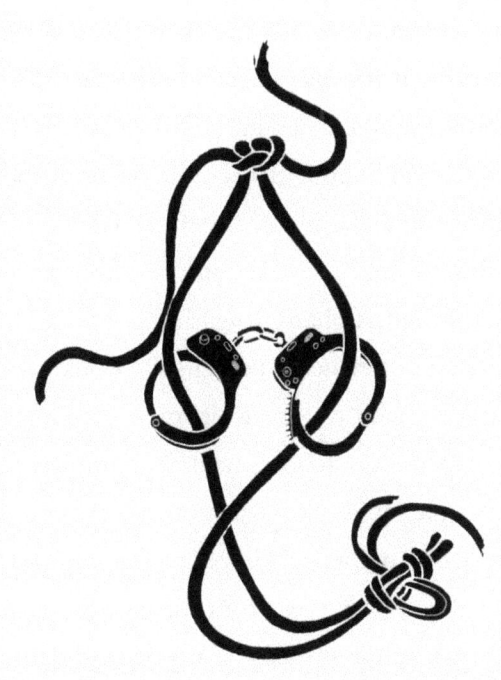

My Lord Lucifer

Hellfire from the Dark Prince's pert hairless bottom (which is intended to be amusing. Before the usual endless tedium about sexism starts. I've spent nearly my entire adult life cohabiting with women. Eight different times. So there's nothing about human misery you can tell me. Sorry, look, women are much better than men. We all know this. The scene is rightly biased towards Fem-Dom as is the universe itself. What follows is a satire on trannies pretending to be women. Written during a very painful time in my life. Which was eventually healed by Ruth Ramsden. A woman. Can I continue now? "Certainly not!" Army of infuriated female supremacists.)

I note that more and more transgender escorts are offering the 'girlfriend experience'. What does this consist of? Is it someone who always thinks the opposite from you, whatever the issue? Is it someone who cares deeply about the tragic deaths of Princess Diana and Kurt Cobain? Whereas you could happily dance a jig on both their graves? Will this girlfriend insist on a choc-orgy watching Titanic while you're just praying for the ship to sink? Do cakes and two hour phone calls to her mother excite her more than hard drugs and hot sex? Then you've got yourself the 'girlfriend experience?'. Perhaps she would sooner spend ten sleepless years arguing with two lively children than have any fun? Then that's the 'wife experience'. (comes with her complete family, free of charge.) Oddly enough you don't see anyone advertising that...

Speaking of the 'wife experience' I have few friends (I know, who'd have thought it?) but two out of these four managed to attract a wife who ran up more than a hundred grand in credit card debts. In both cases it was hard to see where all this money on clothes and beauty products had gone. As they say in the movies, it wasn't on the screen.

Shopping addiction often ends with the guy giving the woman the house and the kids. Oh, and there'll be therapy, buckets of Prozac and lots of hugs for Daddy's poor little girl, who only wanted some retail therapy because her horrid hubby didn't resemble Prince Charming and no one at work had made her Queen. Never mind banning pornography, let's burn every single copy of Cinderella... As bad an influence on women as hardman thrillers are on men.

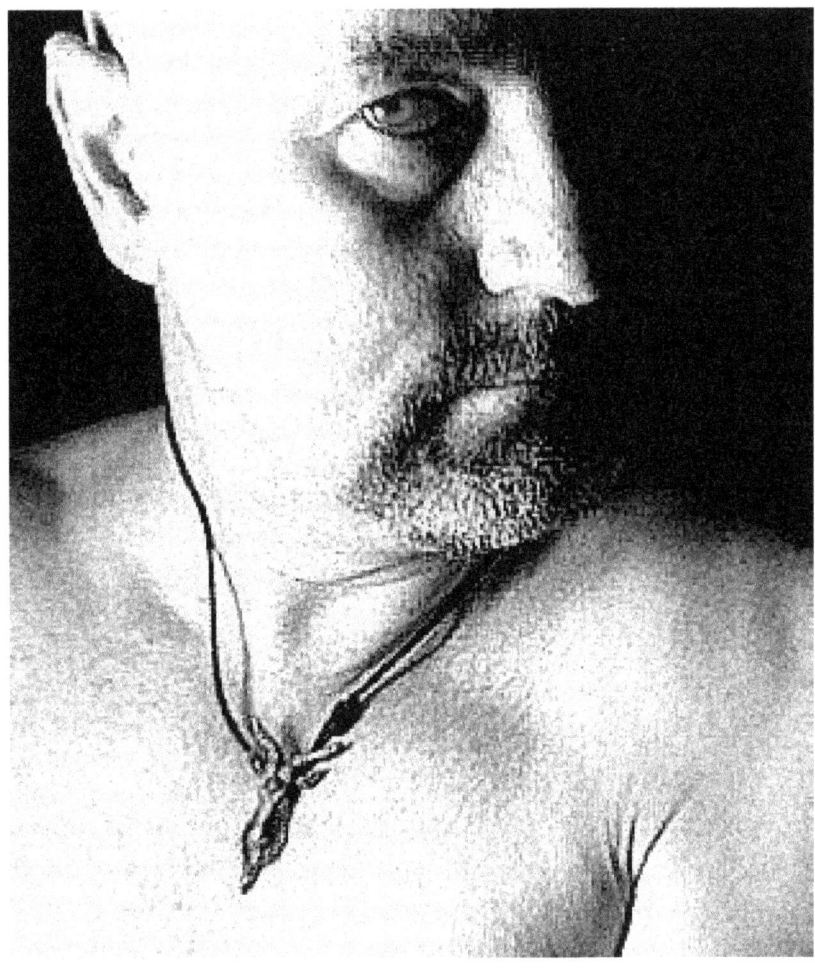

To The Devil A Daughter

As the Lord of Darkness I am currently creating my own female spawn of Beelzebub who will one day torment some poor sap with her own unreasonable demands. Have I dared suggest that a twelve year old might care to listen to what adults say occasionally? Yes, of course. Many times. Has it made any difference? No. Not in the slightest. So while my dear ex-wife spends most of her time shouting and bawling in an attempt to trim the sails of this mini-Domme I'm usually happy to indulge her. Because I prefer enjoying life to endless bickering. Am I creating another monster? Maybe. It's what fathers do. Now if you'll excuse me I have to officiate at an Olympics 2012 meeting. We need more ugly new buildings, instantly obsolescent stadia and some means of getting everyone round this new war zone. We will have total gridlock however much we have to hike the council tax. Or whatever I decided to call it this time. Do you think London's an overpriced kharsi already? Oh ye of little faith. You ain't seen nothing yet...

To get an authentic Satanic flavour I used to write this column on ketamine wearing shiny red boots. After four visits to casualty (two in the same night, I really don't like to be interrupted chasing a good buzz) and one arrest I can no longer continue. From now on I have decided that, rather than access various psychic realms chemically it's safer to invoke Satan himself. The invocation is simplicity itself. Get three tellys and have them all tuned to Graham Norton -that prancing pustule, Satan's leading tormentor on earth - then play some Susan Boyle product backwards while sitting on your biggest and best vibrator. As you chant the myriad names of Beelzebub there will be a sudden puff of smoke, the stench of sulphur and there before you will be the cloven-footed one. He doesn't always like to be disturbed, now he's got a boxed set of

Downton Abbey, but he did agree to ghost this column although there was some nonsense about signing some sort of eternally binding contract. I didn't have time to read the small print but I'm sure it will be all right. We would certainly never descend to the level of fetish fair promoters who couldn't settle their differences in time for the rival London Expos a few year's back. Apparently both beanos were a complete waste of time. Who'd have thought it? As you can see all of the stallholders all year round anyway, and as I see fetishism as a sexual activity rather than an excuse to dress up ("He said WHAT??" Massed Dominatrices from their vanity mirrors) I decided to sit this one out. I did, however, stage my own Expo/Xpo in the privacy of my own home. First I shredded fifteen quid for London parking and fifteen quid for entrance. I then set up some empty tables to represent the exhibitors who didn't bother showing up and I had some foreigners tramp through my living room asking inane questions about fetishism. I had some rude, arrogant Dommes thrust their products and flyers on me, while their pathetic subs slithered behind them. Cue wretched middle aged whining: "Is everything all right, Mistress?" I charged myself four to five pounds for a sandwich and two pounds for a small coffee. Then I shouted and swore at fellow drivers in the slow moving traffic on a computer driving simulator for two hours. Then, exasperated, I glugged a bottle of Jack and went to see my K dealer. I hate trade fairs.

FallenAngelBrewery.com

If you've ever wondered when there will be a range of real ales available in bottles with kinky labels delivered to your door, FallenAngelBrewery.com is the answer to your prayer. Although there's a wide range of flavours and strengths which make these beers desirable it's the stylish. sexy labels which make them indispensable. Lynne Paula

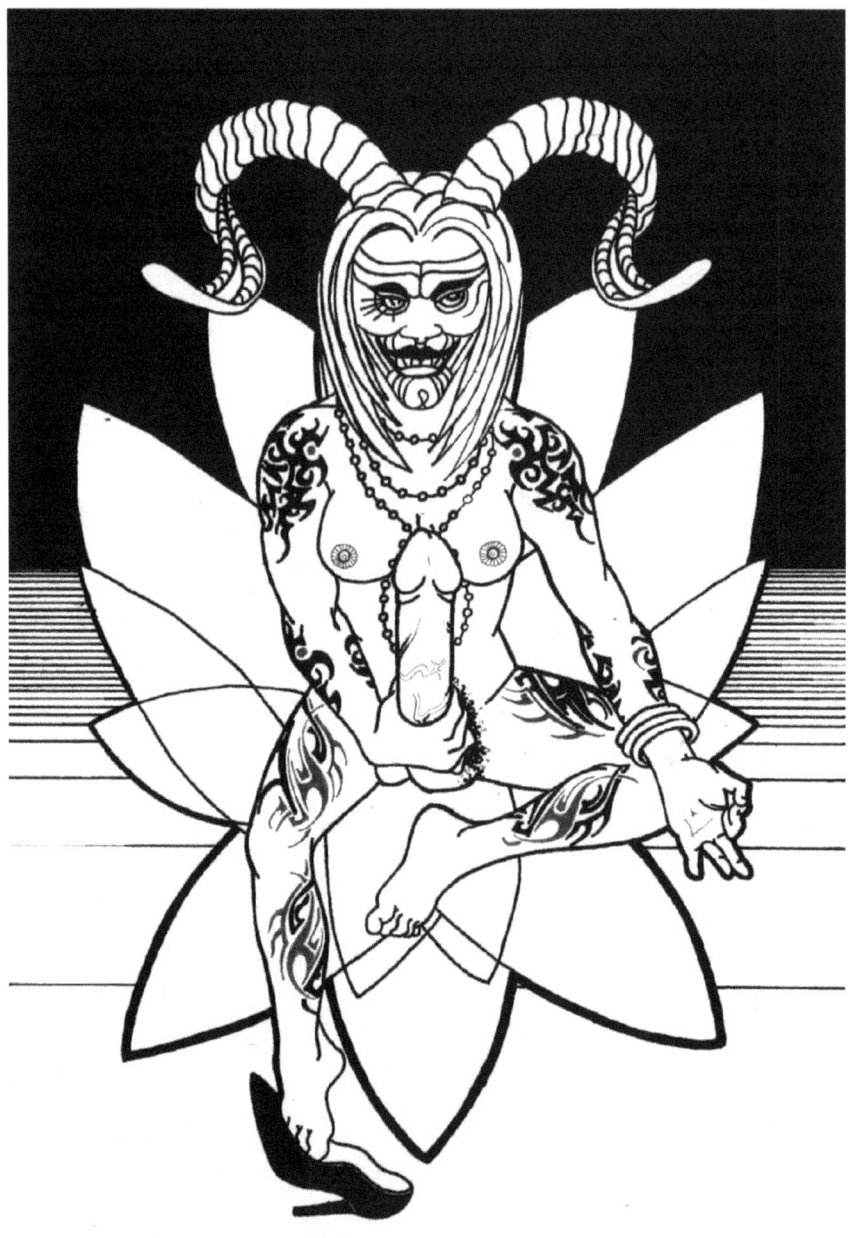

Russell, famed for her upmarket erotic CP drawings for the likes of the Erotic Print Society, has provided FallenAngelBrewery.com with a delicious picture of a bare-bottomed female bent awaiting a birching. Hickory Switch is the only explicitly CP label but there half a dozen others featuring the charms of the female derriere – all likely to be of interest to our readers. There's bare bummed Nuns, bejeaned cowgirls and a Kama Sutra couple practising the oriental art of love. (And I don't mean Leyton Orient. You SLAG!) The sexy, slinky Black Cat label depicts a feline female under a full moon. The flavours include coffee, chilli, honey, malt, hickory smoke, coriander. They even provide discount for War Re-enactors - yet more proof of the crossover between kinksters and another set of loons in leather. Whipmaster Alex Cobra tours the world battling various Vikings and Saxons and was once delighted to be paid by Satanic rockers Cradle of Filth with a freshly forged axe. Rock and, furthermore, Roll. Perhaps more perves should settle their differences with pikes and broadswords. Imagine a charge of whingeing subs. Shuffling along, all whimpering "Let me kiss your feet, Mistress!" And the first Division of Imperial Dominatrices, who haven't quite finished getting ready yet, too busy scratching each other's eyes out to repel the opposition.

Check it out. Excellent beer at a reasonable price and they deliver. Also available from selected outlets in Kent and Sussex. http://www.fallenangelbrewery.com

Sex Toys

Perves who like Family Guy will need "Night-time Lois and Peter", toy rubber-clad fetish versions of Lois and Peter Griffin available online from Mezco. Ltd and sci-fi/fanasy outlets like Forbidden Planet. If you haven't seen it Family Guy contains more pervery than almost any other terrestrial television show while being consistently funny and inventive over many seasons. Incidentally you can take Peter's gimp mask off although you would be well advised not to. And raunchy Domestic Goddess Lois Griffin's ass is not as curvy as it is on the telly. Must have been made by a gay designer. Never mind. She is wielding a riding crop. Peter is brandishing a banana. I have a tireless appetite for anal play but I really don't want to know what Lois is going to do with that banana. The figures come with a background of the candlelit Griffin bedroom. Incidentally, the show's credits will help you stave off the early onset of Alzheimer's. Try learning the name of Thai story editor Cherry Chevapravatdumrong, ideal mental gym practice.

Lovehoney.co.uk

An ethical toy sex store? Do we care? Well, in case I have any tree hugging readers, you can now recycle your vibrators and get a half price new one. They will also donate one pound to some eco-trust, ddjfklkdjlfhgjklf excuse me, my head hit the keyboard as I fell asleep, Getting back to SEX, rather than yoghurt-weaving beardies, they have an excellent selection of ingenious teasers and ticklers, even a realistic faux vagina.(Known as the Piers Morgan). You can see how each product works on their sex toys videos, accessible online. Based in Bath, in five years they have become Britain's leading adult toy independent company. Women need not fear ringing this female-friendly company and they even have a thousand pound prize competition for the best new sex toy you can invent. http://www.lovehoney.co.uk

Vivienne Westwood and Malcolm McClaren

Many fetishists were created by punk when Malcolm McClaren and

Vivienne Westwood took the sexual underground on to the high street. Siouxie Sioux and Gaye Advert must have launched countless men's fantasies and empowered many women to explore fishnets, rubber and sub/dom. True enough but I was just looking for an excuse for my favourite Malcolm McClaren anecdote. A friend of mine was in one of Malcolm McClaren's terrible punk bands on a retainer. As Malcolm liked driving a hard bargain it was often hard to prise their wages out of the crafty old skinflint. Once, when cornered by the band, he came up with this immortal line: "What do you want money for? You'll only spend it."

Reggie Kray And Little Freddie

The last state funeral to be held in Tower Hamlets was when Reggie Kray's funeral cortege was driven with all pomp and circumstance down the Hackney Road to his resting place in, er, whatever that church is called on the corner of Shoreditch High Street. (The wife has done me with a strap on. After a sound yet particularly lewd thrashing. I'm too tired to google.) There was much jostling for position as villains vied with each other to carry the coffin or perform various tasks which would confer upon them a certain standing in the alternative business community. It was an eventful day. A spitfire flew past. Rumours of security consultant and Mark Ramsden lookalike Dave Courtney tooting coke off the coffin apparently displeased the remains of the Kray empire. So we mean no disrespect by pointing out that the first person following the solemn procession of hearses, on his moped, soaking up the grisly grandeur as a fan, was Little Freddie, an infantilist who can be seen getting his bare bottom slippered online by 'Auntie Isobel' www.thediaryofauntisobel.com/ (Video, Stories, Pictures). Freddie, handsome and affable, a true crime fan, hence his position in the cortege,

has been a scene member since somewhere in the mid-nineties, taking a quiet nip of whatever alcoholic beverage is in his baby's bottle and charming an unfeasible number of 'aunties'. What would Reggie have said?

Vampire Eroticism: Rapidly Gaining Ascendency On The Scene

> "Dracula is a kind of incestuous necrophiliac, oral-anal sadistic wrestling match set in a homicidal lunatic's brothel in a crypt."
> A psychiatrist's assessment of Bram Stoker's Dracula.

Alan Davies, the girly comedian, recently sank his teeth into the ear of a London street sleeper, drawing lashings of claret in the process. I actually typed 'Anal' for 'Alan', maybe I should let it stand. Some say drunkenness was the cause of this regrettable lapse. I suspect he must be descended from Count Dracula and was merely peckish. Ordinary mortals stick to kebabs when drunk but the undead may suddenly lunge for the nearest human. Perhaps a tramp's ear is the equivalent of a packet of pork scratchings - good, unpretentious pub fare. It'll keep you going until the right starlet's neck presents itself.

Philip Larkin was a sad old perve, (I'm not being pejorative, it's the truth, as seen by himself). He loved Dracula movies, once writing that he was 'starved of tit and fang'. Fortunately we need no longer rely on sublimated eroticism. Amarantha Knight has written a brilliant erotic version of the Dracula legend, following Bram Stoker's original closely with plenty of fetish and CP action. "Sparing the rod spoils the child of the night." Ms Knight (who writes more respectable material as Nancy Kilpatrik) is a skilful, evocative writer and she clearly loves Kink. If you liked A.N Roquelaire's Beauty trilogy you will like this, which is also considerably filthier. Incidentally, A.N.Roquelaire is horror queen Anne Rice, writing with one hand between her legs. Her work is easier to find than this book, which is part of the Darker Passions series from Circlet press. Dark erotica fans will be able to find Dracula online and in specialist bookstores. Distributed by Turnaround. London has a Vampire society where you can mix and mingle with other bloodthirsty maniacs (surely 'enthusiasts'? Ed). Seriously, there are many who find biting to be an acceptable fetish, a goal in itself. Here's Dr Charley Ferrer, a New York sexologist who hosted a Vampires and Sexual Freedom edition of her radio show. "We explored the beauty of the vampire and its underlying sensuality". She interviewed the creator of Midnight Seduction a vampie role-playing game and was thrilled to have her neck bitten. As ever, dip a careful toe into the water first. Nibble, gently graze the teeth against whatever part of the body you have chosen before proceeding. This is a Marmite fetish, love it or hate it. Incidentally, Goths and Fetishists into the dark side should check out the Alterium.com, the best NO CENSORSHIP site for kinky people of all adult ages and persuasions.

For Your Arse Only: Ian Fleming and Kink

According to a new biography, Fleming was fond of soothing beaten bottoms with cold, wet towels. He beat his wife with canes, slippers and hairbrushes, occasionally receiving from her (as a gentleman should). This fiery partnership also liked endless bickering and making love like scalded wildcats. Passion, perversion and copious amounts of gin weren't quite lively enough after a while so they diversified into adultery. And yet more bickering and make up sex.

I've heard of anaesthetic gel being used after beatings, by receiving

sex workers, although most people like the endorphin high and eventual warm glow. However, an ex-Etonian like Fleming would indeed know how to soothe well beaten flesh. Perhaps he was just trying to minimize bruising, as he seems to have been a bit of a brute. Some players do indeed crave cruelty but far too many tops wade in like Ghengis Khan after eight pints of Stella. It's supposed to be about reciprocal fun, boneheads.

Gordon Brown - A case for non-erotic asphyxiation

Looking for Club Smack's new venue I was surprised to be surrounded by men with chest length beards. I haven't been out for six months but I was still shocked at how quickly fetish fashion can change. And where were the women? It eventually occurred to me that I was supposed to be at 483 Hackney Road not 438, near where a mosque was discharging the faithful.

Back in the 21st century a different sort of worship was available at Images, a smart glitzy club with excellent bar staff and efficient, unobtrusive security. Host Alan was as cheerful and welcoming as ever. He'd made his own Jackson Pollock rubber shirt with some random spurts of paint. ("Random? That's Art, mate!") The resulting riot of colour made me feel a bit drab in fetish monotone. Although Club Rub's Kim certainly had no problem looking stylish and slinky in black. I overheard that the Cockney Knees Up night is unlikely to be repeated, not because no-one liked it, quite the contrary, just because it requires so much planning. Those of us whose efforts are restricted to occasionally managing to stay upright should remember how much work club organisers put in.

Hostess Miranda was oozing sensuality as always. I bought her a

double gin and tonic (in itself newsworthy) and asked what she would like to see featured in this piece. She replied 'your cock'. Well, I wouldn't like readers to feel short-changed so I will just say that this evening was extremely enjoyable, as cheering as one of Miranda's smiles and as wild as one of Alan's belly laughs.

Some say the dungeon play is not as extreme as at certain clubs but then I don't go to a club to see perverts fisting each other. I can get that at home. One guy/girl even came over from Amsterdam for the evening so if it's pervier than that den of iniquity Club Smack must be doing something right.

Like Club Rub, if you arrive without friends you will soon find some. The covered smoking area outside collected some serious conversationalists.

Some fetish guys look like black binbags left out for collection and some look like sex toys for discerning women. Squiggle looked dapper, perhaps helped by being handsome to start out with. I said it was a shame that the more dangerous forms of erotic asphyxiation were becoming more prevalent. It would be nice to see less of it. "Don't hold your breath," said Squiggle. Ho ho. We then agreed that non-erotic asphyxiation was the best way to deal with Gordon Brown .

Tank Girl was enthusing about her man's light up boots, an excellent accessory if you've lost your Lord and Master. According to the ever effervescent TG, fetching and fizzy as always, you only need crawl around until you sight the blinking boots.

Eva Vortex, a gorgeous woman who is also more of a man than most of us, was purring like a pussycat over her latest conquest, an unassuming man who is apparently packing some serious heat in his trousers. As Goddess Eva is stacking a pretty impressive weapon herself, and has tested quite a few in her time, we may take her word on this

matter. A unique combination of heavenly beauty and earthly depravity she has some serious body art and an awesome eye for fashion.

Check her website at Eva-Vortex.com. Among the many hot clips on her site is a vid where she pauses while fisting some lucky lad to blow a kiss at the camera: you won't see many lovelier faces.

Kimmy Bear looked especially cute. I've always liked her 'serious glasses on a fun person' image and don't start me on her pretty face and how alluring her pert bottom looked in skimpy knickers. It was good to reacquaint myself with Miss P, sexy and amusing as ever, one of the few bloggers worth reading, with her handsome geezer, Roo. I never met a nasty Australian and he was no exception. Someone ribbed me for having a hat made out of black kangaroo leather, or maybe it was its Crocodile Dundee name, the Jacaroo. Perhaps kangaroos aren't chic but there aren't any better looking black leather cowboy hats. Unpretentious good value - just like Club Smack. Perhaps I left it a little late for finding play partners but I still managed to have my impudent rump smacked soundly by a lovely black girl, a fetish virgin who was a little shocked at the imprint it left. She's coming back so it will be interesting to see, over a few years, if she turns into an imperious dignity Domme or remains a human being first and foremost.

Absolute power may often corrupt but we can always console ourselves with Club Smack's down to earth clientele. Suck on it fashion poseurs!

The Abba Test

The Marquise is an upmarket lifestyle Mistress with a slight resemblance to Princess Diana (and a trillion more brain cells.) This elegant refined beauty once set me the Abba quiz to see if a man is sub or Dom: which

women would you choose? Well, I might be bisexual but only gay men know the names of the Abba women. But given a choice, I much prefer the blonde. "Dom men prefer the blonde, subs the brunette," she said triumphantly. It works. Try it on your friends.

Perhaps it would also work with The Good Life women. If you prefer fluffy Felicity Kendal you're probably more Dom than those who wish to be crushed underneath Penelope Keith's heels. Marquise.org.uk We once did a photo shoot with me as a shaven-headed, corseted slut groveling on the floor, ignored by the haute couture Goddess laughing triumphantly. Well, I was young and foolish. Now I'm old and foolish it's good to see her still in the saddle. Always on top. She most certainly does not switch, being about as dominant as it's possible to get without establishing your own republic. Hang on, she's even done that: Martopia, where she struts around wearing her personal crest and meting out fiendishly inventive punishments.

Tops who don't switch generally get on my nerves. It's tempting to dream of her receiving six stripes across her impeccably toned little rump but here I'm in a minority. There is an army of sub men who will do anything to serve her so you might have to get in a queue. She's definitely worth it.

If you want more than someone pretending to be a Domme for the money start the long dark journey to the heart of your soul by finding her on Informedconsent.co.uk one of the best online fetish resources. Where I met my dear wife, Ruth Ramsden, author and illustrator of this parish.

The Rimming Machine

A news item on pound coin forgeries mentioned a 'rimming machine'. Which would indeed be a useful addition to any home or office. It reminded me of the comment of one t-girl partner of mine, a rimming recipient. "Oh Ambassador," she purred gratefully, during this deeply intimate tribute, "you really are spoiling us."

Short Story Nick/'Nicola'

"Write something about me," says Nick/'Nicola'.
There are two of us here but this is a threesome. Nick/'Nicola' is two different people; mostly male but also credibly female whenever s/he wants.

'Nicola' is bent over her dining-room table. On huge platform heels schoolgirls shouldn't really wear. With her silver disco skirt rucked up around her waist and translucent red panties hugging her tight, taut bottom. Which is going to get six licks with this rattan cane before being kissed better. After which all heaven may break loose.

But first I'm sat at his/her computer, trying to preserve who s/he is for my own amusement. (And making 'em wait is awfully good for naughty girls).

Capturing who people really are - or at least the way they look to me - is an obsession of mine. Probably because that is the only way you can control anything, That's my inner shrink. A prissy little spoilsport who is also going to get a damn good thrashing in a minute. If I ever get tired of 'Nicola'. And her lovely bum. Which reddens up nicely. Yet always heals quickly. And is so clean inside and out you would think the little darling was an enema enthusiast. But no, she's just delicate.

Sugar and spice and all things nice. That's what this little girl is made of. Sweet as she is, it's often hard to have a relationship with a tranny. They are already deeply committed to an idea of themselves; who they might be - one day soon, when they have found the right wig and make-up. And should I mention relationships in an erotic context anyway? Especially when we are still hot for each other.

The Marquise

We have yet to die the long, slow death of marriage; life without parole, in a cell that's always too small. Couples are, in theory, a union. In practice, they are usually like two dogs fighting over a bone. Or actors elbowing each other out of the spotlight.

"This is about relationships," says Nick/'Nicola'. "It's supposed to be about me!"

Or perhaps like siblings competing for gifts and attention...

The comfort and cuddles brigade sometimes say it is worth getting old and fat together. I was ready for that – for the sake of the children. Whom I love dearly and the pain of missing them is unbearable. But I didn't have enough money for my greedy whore of a wife so I'm back on the prowl now - blade-thin, with an expensive sniffle that just won't quit. Although it's not all bad. I'm permanently excused family Xmasses. And other people's parents.

Nick may not want Xmas but he is still a tranny; a cross-dresser with a hidden agenda. And I'm less interested in being someone else's mirror. Even if s/he is a pretty little thing. Nick has light blue eyes, blonde hair, soft clear skin, a delicate upturned nose and full feminine lips. He is a fine figure of a man. Driving round the countryside in his sports car he looks like the star of a sixties action show. Cruising down the Kings Road in a white Aston Martin. While an acquiescent blonde in a fur coat simpers obligingly in the passenger seat.

Right now he is in his early forties although there are few signs of this on his face. Quite why his skin is so soft and silky is a mystery. No paid liar for the beauty industry would believe that this complexion is the result of a diet consisting of white bread and micro-waved curries. He does not take vitamin supplements or use any grooming products. He washes in supermarket own brand shampoo, a substance also used a shaving lather and sexual lubricant – at least for the purposes of self-love. He's very cute but I doubt whether even he has ever seduced anyone with a handful of cheap supermarket bubbles.

Nick could claim to be trans-gendered, although at an early stage on that confusing journey to two separate destinations - fulfilment both as a man and as a woman. As if those of us setting out in one of those directions ever got far along the road before the traffic got too heavy. Before unexpected diversions eventually sap the will to continue. Besides which, there is only one real destination on this journey, a dark eternal cul de sac that most refuse to contemplate, a lonely old age. Then death. But why not focus on youth and beauty as Nick embodies both those qualities? And, as Philip Larkin demonstrated for far too long, wittering on that we are all going to die is not particularly helpful.

"This is about you again," says 'Nicola'. "Or telling us about some gloomy old git. Write something about me! I'm here right now!"

A proper Dom would have insisted on 'Nicola' saying 'Master' or 'Mistress'. But I can't be bothered taking myself that seriously, being a human first and a pantomime Dom second. He may also be too damn strong to be subjected to real mental and physical torment. Which sometimes pushes people over the edge. I am the dominant partner in some sexual situations, but my hands are softer and gentler than Nick's. I never launched my forehead at the bridge of anyone else's nose. The one punch I ever threw produced a black eye, but it left me with a permanently crooked fourth finger - as no one had ever shown a softie like me how to box.

My grim face sometimes frightens people but Nick actually is rock hard. There have been times when decades of taunts about his prettiness caused a swift and decisive outbreak of violence. Times when ignorant and aggressive drunks found themselves weeping and writhing on the floor, their ugly faces now a little more rugged and manly than they might have wished. Some pretty boys could head-butt harder and faster than the average drunk might have reasonably expected. Maybe 'reason' isn't the right word when discussing the tabloid-fed male, those who judge a sunburnt beer-belly a badge of pride. The media might be liberal these days but your average lad still wants to attack anyone who triggers their buried homoeroticism.

"Write something about me! Not you, again."

She's so needy. Just like me when I was a sub. I rub the twin tails of a tawse between Nicola's legs and watch her squirm as it stimulates some dangling equipment that real girls don't have.

The first time we met I had her over my knee, while others played in the same room. I didn't know her name or anything else about her. For once my dick broke through the drug barrier and a certain shyness during group sex, lurching up towards my belly button. It must have been her mingled earth and sex scent, as I dug my fingers deeper and deeper into her opening. Even though Will was with the gorgeous and beguiling Ritz, he couldn't keep his eyes off us as my hand burrowed in to her past the knuckles. No lube and almost fisting. Scrupulously clean inside and out. Always gagging for it. There must be a flaw somewhere. Oh yes. We both prefer women – heaven knows why, but there it is. I suppose they do offer a better selection of textures and odours. If you can stand the grief.

We both had wives who threw us out although we didn't want to go. And we both didn't want to go for the same reason; the children, whom we love dearly. Neither of us yearn for the dumb dollies we married. Although perhaps Nick and I shouldn't have been dumb enough to listen to society's dictates. Get married! Have children! And if you don't agree you haven't 'grown up'. Although what is so 'grown up' about the adult female search for Prince Charming women have yet to tell us…

"WHY ISN'T THIS ABOUT ME?" asks 'Nicola', justifiably annoyed that s/he had opened so much of herself up and she is being ignored. So let's have some 'back story', as they say in the movies.

His/her mother was still spanking her at a surprisingly late age. This was not exactly child abuse – teenager abuse, I suppose. But if the legacy of these dreadful childrearing techniques is these is these seven hour whip and fuck fests I can't judge her too harshly.

I can't figure out why some trans-gendered people are also tough guys. Did they toughen up in response to fear of being gay? Or did they learn to relax and let the feminine spirit come through as they grew to maturity? I have a shaven head, tattoos and muscles but I have always unconsciously chosen gay or girlie colours, fashions and styles of art. That's Mother Nature and her twisted sense of humour - always eager for a laugh at our expense. Why would she make a fit bloke like Nick then inflict several year's worth of surgery on his manliest organ during the crucial years of adolescence? I couldn't bear to ask why all that surgery had been necessary but the resulting organ eventually functioned well enough to produce two children. Perhaps Mother Nature couldn't make her mind up. Was she building a man or a woman? So she decided to do both.

For a handsome guy he certainly makes a good-looking girl. Especially when 'Nicola' wears my old wig which looks much better on her – a red bob that frames her prominent cheekbones. Seen from behind, like now as she shifts her weight from her aching knees, Nick is an attractive woman with a small, tight tush; a delicate little derriere that most women would do anything for. Anything other than give up alcohol, chocolate and chips. While reserving the right to bitch on endlessly at any other women's slightest gain in weight or the hint of a wrinkle. Oh dear, the writer's a 'misogynist'. No, just pointing out something we all know but aren't allowed to say.

Sometime 'Nicola' reminds me of those perhaps illusory easy to please girlies of my teenage years. Before feminism mobilised and the sex war became about as much fun as a real war. Perhaps I expected too much from women. (Perhaps? Chorus of many disgruntled ex-partners.) If Nick does something annoying it's not like my mother hating me or the pointless random opposition of some women who disagree just for the exercise. It's just a man pleasing himself – which is something I can relate to.

Although it's harder to understand the need to be a woman. For me dressing is another fetish to be explored, another excuse for sexual debauchery. Whereas some find trans-gendered personalities within themselves that strengthen and develop. My female personae come and go, perhaps wilting for the lack of proper care and nourishment.

In my view, not hers, 'Nicola' is sometimes too influenced by those a little too far gone round the transgender bend, a little lost in their own self-built mazes. He talked about hormones, a momentary madness thankfully. For what could be sadder than going through years of gender reassignment to find you don't like your new sex? And you can't re-assign your memories, can you?

Besides, s/he has yet to learn the walk. As for the voice…well, few people get that right and I don't care anyway. The male/female mix is exciting to me. Cross-dressing really is more than an elaborate ruse to allow same-sex eroticism. Cue snickers from lifestyle gay men here, although none will have lasted this far. As this isn't a story about the hunt for the largest cock or the prettiest boy they will probably have turned to something more in tune with their needs and desires. Ooh.

All this cross-dressing must be making me bitchy.

"Stop all this…crap about what gay men supposedly like. Write something about me."

But who are you? You don't even know yourself, for all this talk about dressing being a path to 'who I really am'. And who on earth are 'we', this couple who come together every now and again. We have wildly dissimilar backgrounds so it's hard to see where this could ever go. Without the social glue of ecstasy we would never have met.

"What do you see in me?" s/he once asked.

"You've got many cute habits," I might have said, if ecstasy and ketamine hadn't reduced me to the usual catatonic trance. "Your natural androgyny, that girly face and bum, the way your left eye starts to droop and then stays closed the more blitzed you get. It makes me feel like I must be doing something right. Look! She's winking at me again".

What would he see in me? As I'm not handsome or confident enough. Hardly surprising, as my life has just fallen apart. I'm 'decent', apparently. Which would be news to my wife or anyone else I have hurled a lot of abuse at. But I am a contrast to the many gay men who just want to fuck anything with a pulse then throw it away.

"I WANT TO BE SPANKED. CANED. THEN FUCKED!"

Patience, my sweet. Without me you wouldn't even get on the printed page. Without me you wouldn't have that wig – instead of the foul curly perm you used to have.

And s/he gave herself the wrong name. As trannies sometimes do. I know a posh t-girl called Sharon. And nobody terrestrial should be called Chani, (pronounced Sha-nay). Not that I'm a control freak or anything. Not at all… Chani is a character in a science fiction book and movie. The movie starred Sting. Sorry to invoke the anti-Christ but there it is. Science fiction and a faint memory of Sting. It's definitely the wrong name. So it's 'Nicola' from now on. The name for the person I want to create. Nick may not agree. Couples often don't.

I could rhapsodise about the scent of his, sorry, her body, or some of his cuter habits or just what s/he triggers in me.

But men letching on about their own hunger for sex is not exactly a popular theme so let's stick with the romance Suffice to say I make a three-hour journey each way to get her on my own over a table. Anyone who lives in London already knows that's a pretty strong endorsement.

"Are you STILL writing about me?" s/he asks, wiggling her bum. Which will have to wait for the moment. Fulfilment is transitory but frustration is eternal, my dear…

"Of course I'm writing about you," I tell her, with a fond chuckle. As if I would be going on about myself again. It's not as if either of us are men - selfish bastards concerned only with our own needs and desires.

S/he's right though. It's time 'Nicola' got what she wants. What I want too. And if something doesn't happen soon the reader may well be back on the internet; where you can get anything for free, faster. And there are few enough trans-gendered kink enthusiasts as it is…

"It's not that dragon cane, again is it?" asks 'Nicola'. In a not remotely servile voice. You would never know that 'Nicola' sees herself as a submissive. She's one of the many willing to be a slave, just as long as it doesn't involve any personal inconvenience. And as long as s/he gets everything she wants, when she wants it. Just like I used to be. Luckily I have evolved this Liberal Democrat style of domming. "You might like it if…" "Why not try this?" And I always leave multiple choice options. Perhaps I'm as hopeless as domming as s/he is at subbing. Or perhaps it's infinitely preferable to be who we actually are, rather than follow some tedious, granite-faced s/m script.

"It's the Dragon cane," I tell her. "Rattan. The one with the scarlet thread. And you love it," I tell her, tapping the rod across the proffered buttocks to take aim, prolonging the wait for the first kiss of the cane. And it's another excuse to touch her many more times before the caning begins. Every now and again it's good to pinch her, to ascertain how firm her flesh is, to see how her bottom shifts and wriggles, the cheeks rubbing against each other, occasionally offering glimpses of the mystery in between.

Sometimes s/he yearns to be in a couple. As I do. Although distance conspires against us. And, let's face it. if we lived too close the heat would dissipate. We would have the same problem with monogamy that everyone else has. How often do you want to eat cold porridge? So, for the moment, and in the moment. It's going fine.

"Breathe deeply," I tell her. Although her pain threshold is high anyway. She sometimes complains but she's a pain-slut really. Maybe just an everything-slut, bless her. After a few minutes hand spanking to warm her up it's almost time to begin. She would mark better without the warm up but a caning is a serious business, far too painful without a little preparation. But then she did leave me stranded on the station. In the dark. After I had taken rather too much ketamine, a seriously confusing substance. Especially when consumed on trains. For that she deserves a proper thrashing, never mind 'safe, sane and consensual', the scene mantra which most people ignore whenever it suits them.

It's a fierce joy to peel her red knickers down slowly, to bow down and plant a kiss on each cheek, to catch a hint of her clean but ever so slightly savoury scent. One more swish of the cane through the air, as hard I would like to hit her for keeping me waiting. Which would be painful enough to make her leap up. But I can't do that. Having abandoned senseless cruelty some time in my youth.

There is a deep throaty laugh after the first stroke lands. Is it really going to be that hard? Well, yes it is, petal. S/he loves it anyway. It's best when it's hard enough to feel the next day. When the glow from sex and the shafting with our various toys can still be felt. S/he likes to taunt her homophobic work mates with what a good time s/he has had. Although getting inside her tight, winsomely cute ass is not always easy it's heavenly when I do. But first a disobedient little madam needs her rump reddening.

I stand back and take careful aim. You would never know that caning someone is such hard work, not from pornography often written by people who never do it. It's easy enough to miss and catch someone halfway down the thighs, triggering a searing agony with no erotic benefits.

Another stroke draws a long sigh and a shake of her hips. Then it's time to kneel down and kiss her along the red ridges left by the cane. During which time I lose my head and drift. Lost in the moment. Worshipping her. Pleasing myself. Groaning and grovelling. Sex, violence and religion in one package; how can you go back to infantile dreams of monogamy after this? Pressing her opening with the heel of my hand gets her whole body to rock, preparing her to open up for me later. And all through this my erection is aching. Hello, old friend. Haven't seen you much during the many recent Ecstasy binges. We really must do this more often...

"Write about me!" insists 'Nicola'. Aware that I'm drifting off-message. S/he always wants to be centre stage. Just as I did, when I was in her position. I lay on a few more strokes, which are accepted gratefully. I compare this moment with the many images I have both real and imagined - a resource just as valuable to me as some monogamist's dreams of romance.

Stroke number five falls right across the middle of her lovely cheeks and there is the satisfaction of hearing a genuine cry of pain, something to file away for later enjoyment. I lay on a few more punishing strokes and watch her wriggle. Then I kiss her and help her up. A hug, a cuddle, it's time for a rest. A pit stop to take on fuel before more circuits of the track. More drugs, more depravity. A hint of tenderness now and again. No arguing about sheds, shelves or parental visits. You could get used to this. It's sweet watching Nicola rub her bottom and smiling ruefully.

"It wasn't too hard for you?" I ask, past an age when I might want to use people or hurt them, a veteran of too many broken love affairs and one broken marriage. Which is the only broken marriage I am ever going to have.

"You look amazing," I tell her. "A true Princess."

There was a time when I might have wanted to say 'Goddess' there. Although believing in a female deity that doesn't exist turned out to be no more fruitful than pining for a grumpy old male God.

At some point round about now, when he feels happy or positive about trans-gendered activity, Nick usually says; "I want to be me. I want to be who I really am." The tone is defiant. Perhaps he's addressing his wife or some other ex-partner. I still think that s/he is looking for a woman. As I am, despite it all. Except that she is looking in the wrong place. For real girls often tire of helping trannies find the right wig, the best eye shadow. There may well be women who will put up with not being centre stage; if there is a power imbalance. If there is a significant age difference or if they are doing it for money. Women looking for life partners tend to want raw clay they can mould into something they want. So cross-dressers had better get used to looking for that ideal woman inside themselves. Which may be a sensible strategy anyway.

Tired of chasing genetic girls? Been hurt too often? Think there are too many design flaws in the original product? Well you can always come up with a better prototype yourself. Maybe you already know the love of your life, your own female persona. After all, if you want something doing, sometimes you have to do it yourself...

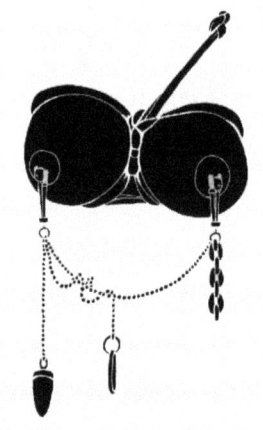

Short Story
Mr Strict - The Diary of a Corrective Therapist

"Love is the only sane and satisfactory answer to the problems of existence". Erich Fromm

Isn't this just like priests saying that God is the only answer? Quite right, my dears, if you don't mind God not existing. Well, I still believe in love. No twelve step group will ever get me to kick it. My clients also live for love. It's a passionate, burning flame. And it's renewed every time they look in a mirror.

The Male Orgasm. Vastly Over-rated? A client orgasms and instantly loses his silly, vacant grin. Oh. Fuck. Back here again. I wasn't sorry to see the high dissipate. Not after a few hours of feverish masturbation and endless wheedled instructions. ('Squeeze my nipples! Squeeze my nipples!'). The guy was Brazilian, perfectly chiselled physically but a little flabby in the brain. He was however impressively focussed on his needs and not shy of communicating them. Occasionally I would tire of squeezing these giant hat pegs as hard as I could. At which point his voice would become whinier and more dictatorial.

'Squeeze my nipples! Squeeze my nipples!' Cocaine makes men even more obsessive and annoying, particularly when they are verbalising very familiar fantasies and English is their second language. This one was still young enough to use it to intensify actual sex rather than as a means of revving the wheels without ever getting the engine in gear. He remained hard throughout the afternoon which eventually became too much like hard work. A barmaid pulling pints for a couple of rugby teams would have had an easier time than I did - wrenching away at that tireless truncheon with little effect. I became a corrective therapist in order to avoid work and here I am getting hot, sweaty and far too bothered.

Did I abandon a promising career in order to yank men's privates around? No, I abandoned show business for love. Although my love of illicit chemicals turned into a marriage made in hell. Actually, why don't I just write 'turned into a marriage'? It's hardly a secret any more how these mutual slavery contracts turn out.

Eventually some thick pre-come appeared and I was able to froth it up into a smoothie. It was hard to suppress a heartfelt "Thank Fuck for that!"

Earlier on, some slow and clumsy roleplay featuring one of his transgendered personae triggered such an intense fit of boredom in me that he was caned much harder than he should have been. But then great hulking geezers wanting to be pre-teen convent girls is about as convincing as an episode of Eastenders. I usually persuade clients that a warm up is infinitely preferable to swift and savage brutality but this one deserved punishment rather than pleasure.

Usually it's possible to trace the severity of a caning by watching red weals blossoming on previously flawless skin. It was hard to know whether I was being too severe and his pain threshold was higher due to drugs. I laid on as enthusiastically as a sexually frustrated nun. Hopefully it would start to hurt when the sex and drug high wore off. As it was the silly grin stayed all the time we played. Then the orgasm triggered sadness, as it sometimes does. The 'little death' is not always fulfilment. For male sex addicts an orgasm means someone's just run off with your stash. Drug addicts discover anew every day that their alternative reality inexplicably disappears leaving them with some crumpled wraps made out of lottery tickets. A sex addict's dream dissolves into the uncomfortable reality of the presence of an unsuitable partner.

At least Mr Hat Peg Nipples, having paid for my services, could discreetly suggest it was time to leave. I had hung around for a good twenty seconds at this point, judging it might be rude to have dashed for the door before he had wiped himself clean but I was already edging towards my clothes and looking forward to an evening gorging myself on Green and Black's Dark Chocolate with Real Cherries. After a two hour soak in a cleansing bubble bath. And the ritual sticking of pins into my Jeremy Clarkson voodoo doll.

This unpleasant little gargoyle is not an accurate representation of that bigheaded bag of poo, just a teddy bear in denims. It's good to have something to vent your feelings on, as I'm sure all wives will agree. Actually, just getting out of earshot of this guy was going to be a form of orgasmic release for me. Coked up clients and their fantasies on an ever repeating ten second loop can quickly become tiresome.

Perhaps too many orgasms depletes the body of zinc, leaving men listless and depressed. or may have done once upon a time in China on their lousy rice diet. Maybe this is why Taoists used to think that semen retention was the path to eternal life. The spermless full body orgasm can be learned in a week, clenching the muscles that stem the flow of urine. Can most men be bothered to learn this? Leave it out, mate! The footy's on! If you already do Kelvins – male pelvic floor tightening muscle tightening exercises – you will find this easier to master. Who says I hate men? I'm giving away information which will make them happier. Those of them who can read anything other than SAS memoirs or computer manuals...

I read Belle de Jour's weblog and find it to be about as credible as a Jeffrey Archer novel. The first post depicts a world where a client quotes from Martin Amis' London Fields and a sex worker recognises the quote instantly. While pigs fly across the sky behind them. Genuine quote follows. ""I want to write my name in come all over you," he said. I smirked. "You can't fool me, you nicked that line from London Fields." He looked at me strangely. Oh no, I thought. Better watch my mouth. "Amis fan?" he said idly, pulling himself with one hand." Genuine quote ends. This putative punter is not the only one pulling himself with one hand here. It's rare to find a woman who wants to read Martin Amis never mind a female sex worker. And a client looking for erotic ideas in Martin Amis? His bleak and pitiless view of sex is more likely to inspire castration than a trip to your local sex worker. And we're supposed to believe this fairy tale? The supposedly cute Bridget Jones twitter soon palls and you will probably want to strangle the nearest kitten. Very pink, very pretty, very pukey.

Sometimes I think clients have a book full of handy hints. It probably reads like this....

> 1. Take enough cocaine to make yourselves temporarily impotent then talk endlessly about this utterly unexpected phenomenon. Then take lots more powders and potions, (Don't worry about the excess poison which will be drained off by heavy sweating. You'll be able to smoke many more cigarettes than usual so make sure you have plenty to hand.)

> 2. Why not take fifteen years off your age on the telephone? This will give me the chance to say, "You're thirty nine? I'm sorry to see that a sudden and unbearable shock has caused your hair to turn white."

I turn few people away and when I arrived at Feeble in Fulham's flat I find it is covered in kitschy poetry, framed and hung at eye level. . "I wrote those," he tells me. "I'm a poet." "Really? What do you think of Philip Larkin?" I ask. "I'm better than him," he says, with no trace of irony or indeed of intellect. He's a poet. Although there's no poetry books to be seen in the flat or any other books, magazines or newspapers. "I wrote several books," I tell him. Which is true. And someone else published them. I didn't have to print them page by page and then hang them at eye level. He has absolutely no interest in this, of course.

But then poets are spectacularly nuts, even by writer standards. This is the dolt who told me he has a 'great body'. Perhaps this is poetic license. The 'great body' turns out to be a fair amount of unstructured flab and a lot of body hair, some of it grey. Presumably it feels 'great' to him. I take out my rattan canes while he talks, sterilise them in front of him. He tells me his disciplinary fantasies. I resolve to fulfil them. It soon becomes clear that he can't even bend over without looking like a collapsing sack of cement. He eventually kneels on his bed while I very gently cane his white doughy buttocks, he can barely take anything above the warm-up. He goes into age regression. He then wants some anal rummaging which I don't particularly fancy as he was too tight to pay for it.

Incidentally, clients, whining is neither endearing or an effective negotiating technique. There's always 'Tyson' though. This black buttplug is as thick as it's vicious, as broad as it's long. Just the job for some punitive anal massage. I have it wrapped and lubed and distending the dolt's rear doorway before he can raise a whimper of protest. There are some moments of deep pleading but even this can't make a man without an erection come. Thirty-Nine? Fifty-something, more like. He asks for a hug. I seriously consider ramming Tyson down his throat but manage some maternal comfort - that is to say, a brief bony clinch and some cold, thin-lipped disapproval. Then it's time to vanish. He lives near a football ground. Which gives me a rare opportunity to see a lot of men with terrible bodies, awful clothes and nasty hair styles all drunk together.

Perhaps my client was right. Compared to this lot he does have 'a good body'. My therapist told me I had many unreasonable demands. Although none were as unreasonable as his bill. At least I provide my clients with a service - physical and mental therapy which actually works. Shrinks get the same money for nodding occasionally and cultivating foul beards which are in themselves grounds for committal. But maybe it's me who needs the strait jacket. What right do I have to attractive clients? In any case, who needs physical beauty when I met a poet who's much better than Philip Larkin? And we had a threesome with him and Mike Tyson.

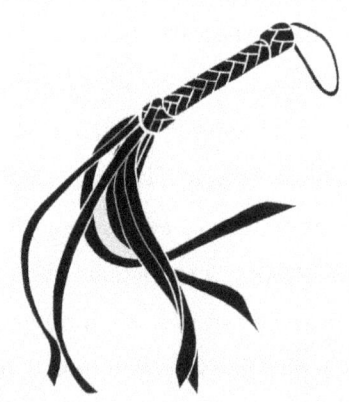

More "Fiction" - The facts are I have found my second and final wife, Ruth Ramsden, artist, author, Goddess, beautiful Sacred Whore - with an hour glass figure and giant geezer-bird brain. Perfection. And she even likes Miles Davis at his most twisted, polytonal, psychedelic best. But this was the 90s...

Madam Petra

Veins full of warm champagne. A warm, honey glow spreading through the midriff. A reason to smile on a grey, winter morning. I never leave Petra's place without fond memories, and a presence that stays with me through the day. This spirit double seems to be compounded of her big pussycat smile, her scent, and her big, beautiful body. Her hour glass figure was once thought to be the ideal female shape – and still is in hotter parts of the world. (And why isn't there a better ready-made expression for 'woman shaped'? You still have to use 'hour glass'. Although we don't tend to measure the time with sand any more).

She has blonde hair hanging in thick thatches down to a joyously deep and full bosom. She's big. Weighty. Broadly luscious and amply bountiful. Big-brained, big-hearted, big-chested and big-mouthed – although she may prefer to be described as assertive. She is a substantial presence, most especially when sat on your face. And hard to miss anywhere else.

She is earthy, rich and mulchy. Fertile soil, which responds well to diligent prodding. Something to dig your fingers into. Real food for real men. Not so much comfort food (the Magnificent Petra is never merely comfortable…) more like the hottest chilli on earth; a meal that challenges you to finish it. Some prefer sushi (or pretend to like it, or need to be seen eating it). But there are times when warriors need to feast. And there is nobody better to gorge upon than the pouting Petra. She is a ten course banquet, washed down by tankards of foaming ale. She is richly rewarding. And fortifying - if you have the strength to take her on in the first place.

Petra and I used to be a guilty secret, then something my wife could join in with. And now we're inseparable. All of us. Cosy as this is, it's not generally a good idea to try to praise two Goddesses simultaneously. If you value your life. So we will leave my wife and Petra snuggled up together for another time. In the fervent hope they will still let me in. It can't be too long before they start to wonder; what do we need the shaven-headed guy for?

Despite her strength and magnificence even Petra has occasional problems with self esteem. Anyone big has to have a problem while too many men seek skeletal woman as trophies. Hoping to enhance their status. Among other drips. But real men feast on flesh. Well, that all sounds bracingly manly; in the old sense of hale and hearty. We just need the drunken cry of 'I am a Genius!', and we might have the start of a Henry Miller pastiche. But it's hard to resist trying to be epic when one is haunted by Madam Petra. Maybe that's the secret; she is not merely human.

How else could a working lawyer learn sword-fighting, hand to hand combat, spell-casting, accurate divination and the extremely esoteric practice of High Art textile weaving? As you enter her boudoir you will be awed by the large loom, a rickety wooden structure that looks more dangerous than the rack of teasers and tweakers hung next to her St Andrew's Cross. Petra produces her art on this contraption, (although most of the public, including me, is more interested in what happens on the St Andrew's Cross). Her textiles perform no useful purpose other than looking interesting - if you know what to look for, and have done a bit of weaving yourself. Even then you still might find the viewing an uncomfortably intense and harrowing experience. But I'd keep it yourself if I were you. She has a bit of a temper. Which is not enhanced by the current indifference of the world in general towards avant-garde textile art. Your average skill-free conceptualist would say, her work is 'merely decorative'. She is 'only' a craftsperson. For whatever reason she never wanted to be a foul mouthed drunk shooting cack-handed videos of nothing much – a reliable indicator of genius in the art business, as we speak.

Her day job is the law, practised for the good of the people, most especially women who have suffered rape and domestic violence at the hands of men. She's been doing it for about twenty years. And a couple of decades watching what happens in the courts and working with the abusers and the abused...she is not short of righteous indignation.

Some of this gets taken out on submissive men and sometimes it is her weaving loom which gets a sound thrashing. The loom is right next to the bed; both wooden structures that creak a lot. If her partners ever pall she swings her legs out from under the duvet and seats herself in front of some hapless fabric and proceeds to rattle out a challenging new creation.

She mutters curses as she weaves - the loom clattering and seething. Germanic magic does involve whispering spells while knotting rope - sometimes around people's necks – but it's best not to know too much about this. There's few enough seekers on the path as it is, without accidental fatalities further thinning out the flock. You may think I'm a bit cowardly for refusing to sample oxygen-deprived sex. I just keep remembering all those guys who get the mathematics wrong – and there are only two seconds in which you can decide whether you are experiencing the best rush ever or is that the grim reaper knocking on the door? Maybe it is. I'll just...Oh. Dear...You may disagree. If so, why not contact the British Auto-Erotic Asphyxiation society? They're usually looking for new members. All you need is the annual subscription and a suit that looks good at funerals.

As Petra weaves, her blonde hair dangles over the whining wood, perilously close to becoming part of the woven fabric. Somehow, she is never dragged into her threshing machine. Perhaps it is because she is a witch – an initiate into most current covens. She has danced with the Druids and swung with the sorcerers. And once you've done all that you are less likely to want to pretend that flower remedies work. Or that your Native American spirit guide is always watching you. Or that 'issues concerning power caused your boiler to collapse' (advice, from a reputable medium, during the cold snap of 2001). Let's face it, If New Age remedies fixed anything, sweet Diana Spenser would have been well. Instead of quite ill.

Some flowers get trodden underfoot but no-one is going to step on Petra. She is a warrior - hot words and cold steel. After a few years with Petra it was becoming clear that all this crusading lawyer stuff is a just a cover story. She is actually one of the three Germanic Goddesses. Petra is the one who weaves the future. If ever your life seems to be sabotaged by an unseen assailant you can always blame her – Petra, the weaver. Your Viking warriors would sometimes cite Loki as a trickster God - it came in handy when far too many of the opposition turned up and overwhelmed the lads with the horned helmets. But it's not him – grumpy old blokes with beards are less in demand these days. You can put sudden reversals of fate down to the Weaving Woman. The loon with the loom. Her. The Goddess. Petra.

As a long-time playmate I was recently invited to watch her favourite tranny slave serve tea. I was wearing a dark Ozwald Boateng jacket with a thin red pinstripe, a shimmery lilac houndstooth shirt by Thomas Pink and some charcoal trousers that seemed to cost far too much at the time. I mention this lest anyone suspect I had attempted to cross dress. Not that I haven't tried. Who wouldn't want to be dressed up in Madam's extensive theatrical wardrobe? But we eventually gave up on the attempt to feminise me. I tend to look like a biker's bitch or a rock chick who can't quite kick Jack Daniels. It feels great. But it looks terrible. So I leave all that to 'Tracy' these days, Madam Petra's most faithful slave.

Mistress/slave relationships often crash and burn. Slaves are usually far from slavish in their demeanour, often demanding far more than they deserve – or offer in return. "Do I really have to care about someone's emotional health just to get my dishes done?" asked Ruby, another Domme who is always looking for slaves to manage her domestic chaos. Indeed so. You might as well be married, my dear. So this must also be in praise of Tracy, a good looking bloke who makes a better looking woman. And actually behaves like a slave, instead of an Argentinean Dictator whose shoes don't quite fit. As many of his rivals do. Tracy's thing is forced feminisation. Punished in panties. But it is doubtful whether we should use words like 'punishment' for this process. It often appears to involve a greedy little slut getting what he really wants. Or it may be having a license to be a slut for a few hours. Even better, someone else is forcing you to do it. So you get to do what you want, except that it is someone else's fault. No more decisions, or responsibility. A holiday from who you have to be to cope with the outside world.

I first knew Tracy in the context of a five way exchange of sexuality in a night club. She was on all on fours offering herself to those approved by Madam Petra. It was hard to ignore Tracy's immaculate rump, two peach halves immaculately clad in flawlessly white panties. Tracy arrives at clubs looking like a sixties pop goddess; thigh boots, mini-skirts, hair reminiscent of Sandie Shaw. As a French Maid, dressed for service, she is even more attractive. It sometimes seems a shame that someone of refined birth and exquisite manners should be lumbered with 'Tracy' (it's a tribute to a former Mistress). But perhaps this humiliation is exquisitely painful for such a delicate flower, a further way of revelling in being downtrodden.

Tracy managed to serve Petra and I tea, behaving impeccably despite Madam Petra's lewd banter and wandering fingers. But it wasn't long before her impossibly high standards required that punishment be administered. Perhaps she thought Tracy was flirting with her guest. The little minx did seem to be over-hospitable with Madam's gentleman caller. And Madam does not like being ignored, even for an instant. There is only one God. And her name is Petra.

"It is obviously far too long since I have punished you," said Petra. "You filthy little slut."

"Yes, Madam. Thank you, Madam." Tracy leaned forward, offering herself, big eyes imploring. Petra smiled, all too familiar with her slave's little fads and fancies.

"I know you want to be over my knee," she said. "But this is a punishment. Your head would be far too close to my shiny black stockings. It would be far too easy to drink in Madam's scent."

We were already gratefully aware that Madam was wearing Angel by Thierry Mugler. And that it was floating around the room on a cloud of sex hormones pulsing from her gorgeously fleshy body. Tracy turned away from the face she so adores and bent to touch her toes. Madam flipped Tracy's skirt up and patted the seat of her knickers.

"I'm relieved to see you have grasped the concept of whiteness at last. My arm ached for two days last time. Not as much as your bottom hurt though, did it?"

Someone else was with us now. A firm but fair Matron who will stand no nonsense. Petra can credibly impersonate Marilyn Monroe, a stuck-up Duchess, a Victorian streetwalker, wenches in general and teenage minxes in particular (with choice of regional accents and accurate period detail. Favoured epochs; Victorian, Restoration, Dark Ages). And her bossy lady with slutty little slave is absolutely flawless. But then so it should be, after all these years.

She checked Tracy's posture, straightening one of her legs before patting the seat of her knickers approvingly. She reached for a wooden spoon, an implement chosen to emphasise domestic servitude as well as an effective tool for inflicting of bruising, scorching pain. She stood and measured the spoon against her target, using it on each cheek in turn, taking time out to examine her slave's flushed face, to pinch her nipples. The punishment became more intense. Soon there was a fierce red glow visible through the thin white panties. Although Tracy was silent her breath came thick and fast. There was an occasional sigh as the spoon thrashed the same spot repeatedly.

"You may stand," murmured Petra eventually. She was flushed, a faint moist glow on her formidable cleavage.

"Thank you, mistress," said Tracy, sincerely. She curtsied as Petra has taught her, although there was the occasional unavoidable squirm as Madam's lecture continued. Finally she held the spoon for her to kiss. Eyes downcast, Tracy planted a long kiss on the implement before Petra took her chin by its point and tilted it upwards. She stared down at her slave for a while, imprinting her dominance deep inside her. Then Petra clutched the bulging erection in Tracy's knickers, kneading and massaging the throbbing mound. While the sighing slave jiggled from foot to foot. We watched her hop for a while. It was entirely cute.

"You may rub yourself," granted Petra. Tracy mewled in relief as she strived to lessen the harrowing sting in her well-beaten bottom. It was some time before she recovered her composure. She then needed considerable strength and endurance to comply with the rest of Madam's most unreasonable demands. Never able to forget that failure meant another punishing session with the wooden spoon.

When Petra was satisfied she had pushed her slave just that little bit further than last time, she gave Tracy some more domestic tasks. And we were free to talk once more. Assam tea arrived. A strong, full-bodied brew. Just right for a strapping lass like Petra. It even sounds like s/m. As we sipped at its dark strength I asked Petra if I could write a story about her.

"I thought you were burnt out," she said, with a smile appropriate for this piece of self-pitying amateur dramatics. "Why write 'another erotic story'?"

I let her mock me for a moment. Which is fair enough, considering how much material there is to work with.

"It might be nice to bring a beautiful women alive," I said, hoping that it would please her. She smiled. And glowed. And we felt the space enclose us. Sometime, somewhere, we are always together. Exchanging fragments of dreams and whispered prayers. In the long, slow, sweet dance of desire. Warmed by a pussycat smile.

21st Century Eddie Drood – Charles Dickens Remixed

Zero, a young documentary maker and skateboarder is a guest in Mr Madden's Rochester dungeon. He captured her by mistake. He cannot kill women, only Chavs and male paedophiles. They are discussing the best online fetish community.

"Look on 'Informed Dissent'," says Zero, waving a patronizing hand at me, thinking I won't have heard of this excellent pick up site, sorry, valuable community resource for Kink enthusiasts. Au contraire. Gawd bless whoever's in charge because I've found several partners through it and many useful hints on toys and technique. I find the site referenced by Zero and discover it is still the usual collection of Asperger's sufferers, and the extremely thin skinned, who nevertheless insist on heated debate of minutiae more suited to trainspotters or, saddest of all, those who write down the numbers and types of busses. You're also left with the impression that the s/m community is now almost entirely male worms looking for farcically exaggerated forms of abuse - ballbusting anyone? Actually being kicked as hard as possible in the unprotected testicles by mad harridans? Don't we get enough of that anyway? Metaphorically? Well, the balance of power is shifting ever further towards fem dom in civilian life, as it should. We do need equality. But do we need a kicking in the nuts? Train Robber Bruce Reynolds was once held down by warders who took it in turns to kick him in the balls. If only he had known he was a fetish pioneer. Then there's a generous helping -appropriately enough as many are morbidly obese – DISCLAIMER! I've had many large partners and they were all lovely, seriously, before someone kills me, there's nothing as hot as a big woman radiating heat, sex, love and mad erotic power. Ahem. There's more than an adequate sufficiency of angry women, of all shapes and sizes, and various personality disorders, all going hogwild having finally found a soft target that won't strike back.

    I knew someone who was such a user that a man pretended to be dying to get rid of her. Without success. She would have relationships just to get the bathroom grouted or the rockery moved. Fine, if the promised thrashing is delivered, social pariah status if it doesn't. Enough sermonizing. I've got Chavs to kill.

The Meaning Of Life

"An Unfashionable Hobby For Many Wizards. With a simple wand and chalice you can perform the most chaotic conjuration of all – launch an entirely new person, and thus cheat death and throw bombs at the future."

Pete J Carrol, *Psybermagick*

The purpose of life is to reproduce, hence the importance of sex to human beings. However, fetish sex or any other form of radical desire often has nothing to do with reproduction. It produces extremely intense experiences but, due to the transitory nature of the scene, an act may not bond a pair of partners together – it may be committed purely in order to celebrate the moment. The sense in which romantic sex strengthens a couple is missing.

I discovered psychedelic drugs and pornography before I ever had sex with anyone. In the early 1970s this was perhaps a strange order for these important rite of passage experiences but is now much more common. The idea of using sex to make babies was then completely irrelevant for me during the next few decades. I was in my middle thirties before I even contemplated having children. And after more than two decades of sexual activity the idea of copulating in order to produce a baby seemed odd, a bit *kinky* even. It was an odd and not entirely comfortable feeling to pause before an act of intercourse and consider the myriad possible futures. I have committed many supposedly 'deviant' acts in the pursuit of radical desire. I have experienced fear and transcendence, joy and terror but the most radical act of my sexual life was undoubtedly that of intentionally creating another human being.

The Author Recommends

Mistress Demonic: Sweet, salty, pant-wettingly funny, also one of the most serious skilled Mistresses around, particularly in medical matters. http://www.MistressDemonic.com" www.MistressDemonic.com

Master Keith partner of Mistress Demonic: One of the very few men who are expert Masters, cool dudes and funny as fuck. Also a scene pioneer. The Gate Club simply must be visited. http://www.thegateclub.co.uk" www.thegateclub.co.uk.

ClubRub.com and Kim Rub: A superb night out for rubberists, dancers, fun fetish people. Kim is a gorgeous, friendly hostess. Even better since I've been banned.

Sidonia Von Bork: Heart-stoppingly beautiful and smart top class blonde mistress. Runs http://www.theenglishmansion.com. The best, hardest fem dom anywhere.

TortureGarden.com deserves its worldwide renown. Still fashion forward, indeed scarily avant garde. A total mind fuck.

Empress Victoria: Highly intelligent & creative oriental Mistress.

The Marquise: Goddess. As beautiful as Princess Diana, there's a slight resemblance if I may say so, but a thousand times cleverer. Contact *respectfully* through www.InformedConsent.co.uk.

Madame Caramel: Superb Big and Beautiful black women behind the excellent night out www.theblackwhip.com where Mistress Kia, a lithe lethal beauty may be found.

Eva Vortex: More of a man than most of us and a gorgeous woman too. Pre (no) op transsexual. (It would be a crime to remove that mighty weapon.) Creative body artist and scene legend. www.eva-vortex.com.

I know nothing about rope, the fetish du jour. This man knows just about everything. Shibari expert Bruce Esinem. www.esinem.com.

SkinTwo.com The best rubber fashion and fetish magazine ever. Hail Tim Woodward, there at the start. We are not worthy.

ChinaHamilton.com If you like female bottoms, CP, beautiful women and superb compositions Mr Hamilton's your man. A master of chiaroscuro.

Trevor Watson. Excellent and daring fetish photographer, (translation, very rude pics in unauthorised locations. His 'Cheek', focussing on the female derriere is an essential purchase.

Alex Cobra, Whipmaster: A quick quipper who makes beautiful corporal punishment equipment in addition to being an artist with the bullwhip. A little like being whipped by a fetish Blackadder, but he's very serious when it comes to providing the best kit. www.cobrawhips.com.

CoffeeCakeandKink.com: Was a brilliant cafe and art gallery, now online source of toys and much more.

Tied and Teased: Excellent fetish and contact magazine. www.tiednteasedonline.com

Apologies to all the many experts who are not listed here. These are the people, places and resources that have made the strongest impression on me since I set sail publicly in 1992. And if you're worried about taking the plunge for the first time, come on in, the water's just fine.

A Witch's Guide To Sexuality & Good
Relationships By Tarona Hawkins
& Howard Rodway
ISBN 978-1-906958-14-5, £11.99

Four years ago when I was discussing the subject of natural healing with practising witch Dr Tarona Hawkins, she mentioned during our conversation that she had notes, files and first draft chapters prepared about her psychic readings, counselling, past life regression work, magickal treatments and herbal remedies, all relating to clients' sexual problems.

Tarona Hawkins added that her reputation as a sex witch had gathered such momentum that most of her time was now occupied with sex counselling. This volume is the end result of accepting Tarona's invitation to transform her records and her knowledge into *A WITCH'S GUIDE to SEXUALITY and GOOD RELATIONSHIPS*.

Within this book you will find covered an incredible variety of sex and sex related subjects, for example: Sex magick, sex massage, adult babies, fetishism, demonic sexual encounters, group sex, homosexuality, anal sex, sadomasochism, transvestism, transsexualism, sex feeders, sex for the elderly, impotence, penis enlargement, male hygiene, menstruation, past life traumas, the human sexual aura, sexual handwriting characteristics together with other sex related subjects.

To all those who read this book; individual members of the public, those with sexual problems, sex counsellors, and of course the occult community, it is hoped that through this book new insights will be gained into the unusually varied spectrum of human sexual behaviour.

Order direct from
Mandrake of Oxford, PO Box 250, Oxford, OX1 1AP (UK)
Phone: 01865 243671 (for credit card sales)
Prices include economy postage
online at - www.mandrake.uk.net